TORT CONTRACT LAW

JOHN LOK

Contents

Foreword

The common law tradition, shared by the United Kingdom and the United States, serves as the bedrock for the modern law of obligations. While both jurisdictions trace their lineage to the same historical roots—the English courts of the medieval period—the evolution of Tort and Contract law in these two nations has been marked by a fascinating divergence.

This work explores the interplay between these two pillars of civil liability. In the United Kingdom, the law has remained largely tethered to a tradition of incremental judicial development and parliamentary sovereignty. Conversely, the United States has seen a more experimental approach, characterized by the influence of the Restatements, the constitutionalization of certain tort principles, and a distinct emphasis on economic efficiency and social policy.

By examining the doctrinal nuances of duty, breach, and remedy in both jurisdictions, this book seeks to illuminate not only how these systems differ, but why they continue to converge in their shared pursuit of justice. It is intended for the practitioner and the scholar alike, providing a comparative lens through which to view the enduring relevance of the law of obligations in a globalized legal landscape.

Preface

Introduction

Overview of UK and USA Business Law

The United Kingdom and the United States have distinct business laws, shaped by their unique histories, cultures, and judicial systems. Understanding these differences is crucial for businesses operating in both countries.

Employment Law

UK employment law provides more protection to employees than US employment law. In the UK, employees are entitled to prior notice of termination, and employers must provide a written statement of employment terms within two months of the start of employment. Additionally, UK employees with two or more years of service have a statutory right not to be unfairly dismissed.

In contrast, US employment law is generally more employer-friendly. The US does not recognize the concept of "at-will" employment uniformly, but it is widely practiced.However, this concept allows employers to terminate employees without cause or notice, which is not the case in the UK.

Contract Law

UK and US contract laws have different requirements for contract formation and enforcement. In the UK, contracts must be in writing, and employers are required to provide employees with a written statement of employment terms.In the US, contracts can be verbal or written, but written contracts are generally preferred.

Corporate Governance

UK corporate governance is based on a principles-based approach, which provides flexibility and considers the specific circumstances of each company.In contrast, US corporate governance is rules-based, which can be more rigid and punitive.

Intellectual Property Law

UK and US intellectual property laws have similarities, but there are also differences. For example, in the UK, copyright law provides protection for the life of the author plus 70 years, while in the US, it provides protection for the life of the author plus 75 years.

Litigation

UK and US litigation systems have distinct differences. In the UK, the loser pays the winner's legal fees, while in the US, each party typically pays its own fees. Additionally, US courts allow cameras in courtrooms, while UK courts have historically been more restrictive.

Taxation

UK and US tax laws have different approaches to corporate taxation. The UK has a corporate tax rate of 19%, while the US has a federal corporate tax rate of 21%.

Conclusion

In conclusion, UK and US business laws have significant differences in employment law, contract law, corporate governance, intellectual property law, litigation, and taxation. Businesses operating in both countries must understand these differences to ensure compliance and success.

This book explains what are tort and criminal and contract law basic elements and indicates some case studies questions and suggests answers to let readers to know whether what are the real tort and contract and criminal law function. It is suitable to any professionals , e.g. accountant, lawyer, doctor, architects. They may know whether how they ought do to avoid to do any wrongdoing behavior in order to avoid to compensate any tort liability to their clients. Also, any law students and people who have interest to learn tort law, this book can provide any basic tort and criminal and contract elements knowledge to let them to know.

Prologue

CHAPTER ONE

Tort law

(1) Tortious acts many be classified in what ways?

Tort law refers to the set of laws that provides remedies to individuals who have suffered harm by the unreasonable acts of another. The law of tort is based on the idea that people are liable for the consequences of their actions, whether intentional or accidental, if they cause harm to another person or entity. Torts are the civil wrongs that form the basis of civil lawsuits.

An area of law that deals with the wrongful actions of an individual or entity, which cause injury to another individual's or entity's person, property, or reputation, and which entitle the injured party to compensation. They may include intentional tort refers , when a person intended the results or consequences of the act, e.g. assault, battery or false imprisonment; strict liability refers , when a person's conduct was neither intentional nor negligent, but is held liable wothout the plaintiff needs to prove fault; negligence refers when a person is careless, e.g. if a defendant decides to throws a stone at the plaintiff, the defendant has committed an intentional tort. But if the defendant intentionally throws a stone at a tree, buy misses and hits the plaintiff, the defendant may be negligent. Other torts included frequently enountered by the general public and include such acts as nuisance, occupier's liability, trespass and defamation.

Tort is conduct that harms other people or their property. It is a private wrong against a person for

which the injured person may recover damages, i.e. monetary compensation. The injured party may sue the wrongdoer (tortfeasor) to recover damages to compensate for the harm or loss incurred.

The conduct that is a tort may also be a crime.

Some torts require intent before there will be liability and some torts require no intent. In other
words, in some cases, there is liability for a tort even though the person committing the tort did not have any intent to do wrong.

● Types of Torts

There are basically three types of torts: intentional torts,torts based on negligence and strict liability torts. An intentional tort is a civil wrong that occurs when the wrongdoer engages in intentional conduct that results in damage to another. Striking another person in a fight is an intentional act that would be the tort of battery. Striking a person accidentally would not be an intentional tort since there was not intent to strike the person. This may, however, be a negligent act.

Careless conduct that results in damage to another is negligence. The intent element of these torts is satisfied when the tortfeasor acts with the desire to bring about harmful consequences and is substantially certain that such consequences will follow. Mere reckless behavior, sometimes called willful and wanton behavior, does not give rise to the level of an intentional tort.

If a person commits an intentional tort, this means that he intentionally violated a legal duty he owed to the victim. This is different from a negligent tort, in which the tortfeasor violated the duty that every member of society has to exercise reasonable care in their actions with others.
The distinction between an intentional tort and a negligent tort is important for several reasons.

First, if an individual wants to sue for an intentional tort, he must prove that the tortfeasor acted with "intent." This is a separate legal requirement that the plaintiff must fulfil, in addition to proving all the other facts of the case and proving actual damage. Strict liability, sometimes called absolute liability, is the legal responsibility for damage, or injury, even if the person found strictly liable was not at fault or negligent – the injured party is not required to prove fault – liability is strict. An example of strict liability is injury caused by wild animals in the care of the tortfeasor; because the tortfeasor owns tigers, the tortfeasor is responsible for any injury, without the need for the injured party to prove negligence.

(2) What does tort of negligence mean?
The tort of negligence is the right to protect one's self and one's property from harm caused by the unreasonable behavior of another. Negligence

is defined as careless or lack of proper care and attention in performing some act. A person is negligent as a tortfeasor, even if that person did not intend the consequences of the act (injury to another person or damage to another's property). It means that the tortfeasor was unaware of negligence of his action.

Negligence is as a tort m it is a breach of a legal duty to take care which results in damage to the claimant. It has four elements of negligence on a claim against a tortfeasor as below:
The defendant owes a duty of care to be injured party, i.e. a legal duty rather than a moral duty, the defendant must have breached the duty of care owed to the injured victim, who is bringing the claim to court, the victim's injury or damage must be caused by the defendant's breach of the duty of care, i.e. causation and the victim must suffer injury or damage.
    (3) What does breath of duty of care mean?
It means that the conduct that falls below the standard regarded as normal as desirable. The special relationships may include: common carrier to passenger, innkeeper (hotel, motels) to guest, employer to employee, landowner or possessor to invitee, teacher to student, parent to child, hospital to patient, a professional person, such as a solicitor to client and lifeguard to swimmer. They have special duty of care roles to their clients.
The evaluate whether the defendent has breach of the suty of care. It depends on determining foreseeability factors as below:
Area in the location of the event and its physical nature, activity means the types of activities, which were present leading up to the event, people means the type of individuals involved in those activities, which lead up the event, human nature assumption means that the type of behavior which may be expected from those participating in the activities , participation means the anticipatory actions which were taken prior to the activities, historical data means where there was any prior knowledge of similar to identified occurrence and common sense factors.

● Duty of care
    The defendant in a negligence action must have owed a legal duty of care to the claimant. There is a three-stage test to establish whether there was a duty of care:
    · Is there a relationship of proximity between the parties?

· Was the injury to the claimant foreseeable?
· Is it fair, just and reasonable to impose a duty?

● Breach of duty

For the tort of negligence to have occurred, the defendant must have breached the duty of care legally imposed on them.The 'reasonable man' test is usually applied to ascertain whether the duty of care has been breached. This is a objective test, and considered whether the behaviour of the defendant fell below the threshold of a "reasonable man".

This will vary depending on the nature of the defendant. For instance, in a medical negligence case following a surgical procedure, the 'behaviour' – ie. the skills – of a specialist surgeon will be expected to be of a much higher standard than the skills of a junior doctor assisting. However, inexperience of itself will not be a valid defence: the defendant is expected to discharge his or her legal duty as a reasonably skilled and competent person.

● Causation

Once a breach of the legal duty of care has been established, it must be shown that the loss, damage or personal injury was caused
as a result, whether directly or indirectly. The question is: but for the actions or omission of the defendant, would the loss or harm have resulted?

● Harm or injury

There must be some form of loss, damage or injury. This includes physical or mental personal injuries; financial loss; or damage to
property. It can also extend to emotional distress or embarrassment.

(4) What does damage mean in tort of negligence?
Damage is the actual harm or loss suffered. Damages are the compensation which the injured party seeks from the tortfeasor. Damages frequently involve the issue of the actual amount of an injured party's financial loss. Generally, tort law is intended to make the injured party " whole" again, e.g. an award of damages is to serve as compensation for the losses.
What do damages mean in tort law ?
There are two types of damages recoverable, general and special damages both types. General damage is damage said to be the result of the tortious act complained of and need not be specified pleaded. Special damage means the particular damges, beyond the general damage, which results from the particular circumstances of the case.
Tort law is the body of laws that enables people to seek compensation for wrongs committed against them. When someone's actions cause some type

of harm to another, whether it be physical harm to another person, or harm to someone's property or reputation, the harmed or injured person or entity may seek damages through the court.

Damages are a monetary award ordered by the court to be paid to an injured party, by the party at fault. Damages may be awarded in compensation for loss of, or damage to, personal or real property, for an injury, or for a financial loss. The types of damages that may be awarded by the court for civil wrongs, called "tortious conduct," of an individual or entity include: Reimbursement for property loss or property damage, medical expenses, pain and suffering, loss of earning capacity and punitive damages.

(5) How to denfence to the tort of negligence?

The tort law may involve both a civil case and a criminal case resulting from the same act. IN a civil case, the burden of proving liability is lower than in a criminal case usually. The injured part in a civil case must prove all the element of the tort of negligence on the balance of probabilities standard. Otherwise, if the injured victim has failed to prove its case and the defendant is free of liability .

A tortfeasor may raise a defence which would relieve the tortfeasor from full or partial liability for the injury caused to the victim. Defences available to a tortfeasor against a claim of negligence are mainly contributory negligence and assumption of risk.

At common law, the defence os contributory negligence could completely prevent an injured victim's court action, provided that the victim was unreasonable in avoiding risks, and if this unreasonableness was a substantial factor in producing the injury. This would be the result, even if the defendant was also negligent.

On other words, if some contributory negligence could be shown on the injured victim's part, the victim would not be able to claim any damages in a negligence action. Assumption of risk means no injury is done to a person who consents to the risk of injury. It is a complete defence to an injured party's lawsuit. If a victim knowingly and voluntarily accepts the risks of injury by the defendant's negligence, the injured party can't recover for any loss, damage or injury . Courts generally interpret this denfence as courts are on policy to deny a victim of any compensation.

In addition, the concept of negligence has undergone significant reinterpretation over time, according to legal scholars. The law now takes into account the fact that manufacturers often have more ability than consumers to avoid accidents; thus, it is more likely to view failure to take inexpensive action as negligence or to attach liability to indirect or partial contribution to an injury.

(6) What may be included to tortious liabilities?

The legal term tort refers to an action in which one person or entity causes injury, harm, or damage to another person or entity. A tort liability may occur as a result of intentional acts, a negligent act, a failure to act when the individual had a duty to act, or a violation of statutes or laws. The individual who commits the tortious act (the act leading to the tort liability claim) is called the "tortfeasor," and is the defendant in this type of civil lawsuit. Such a defendant is generally held liable for damages or harm suffered by the plaintiff, as a result of the defendant's acts.

In many tort cases, the damages or injury suffered by the plaintiff do not have to be physical injury. A defendant in a tort liability case, who is found to be liable for his or her tortious acts, may be ordered to pay damages for harm, such as violation of personal rights, pain and suffering, and emotional distress.

Tortious liabilities may include employer's liability, breach of statutory duty, employer's liability to workers, occupier's liability, nurisance, trespass, defamation. Vicarious liability is legal responsibility imposed on a person for the torts of others, regardless of any fault on the part of the non-tortfeasor. Vicarious liability generally arises from an employer and employee relationship and is conceptually similar to strict liability in tort.

Under vicarious liability , an employer's liability does not depend upon the employer's person fault. Rather, an employer is strictly liable for an employee's negligent acts performed of employment . The requirements for vicarious liability are the tortfeasor is hired by the employer as an employee , the employee committed the tortious act, the employee's tortious act was in connection with, or employment, e.g. employer's liability for independent contractors. IN general , employers are not liable for torts committed by their independent contractors. The most basic principle is that an employer is not liable for an independent contractor's negligence, provided always the contractor employed is one reasonably supposed by the employer to be competent.

Trespass is unlike negligence, involves an intentional act. Trespassory tort, such as trespass to the person or trespass to land, are less frequently than the negligence-based torts. Then committed this type of tort often is also a crime for which the wrongdoes is imprisoned. Acts such as murder and rape are examples of trepass to the person, but are usually only dealt with as criminal acts by courts. Therefore, an injured party would not bother with the inconvenience of a civil action, although the right to sue exists, e.g. hospital negligent medical treatment to patients case.

Defamation is a tort action for the protection of one's reputation to establish defamation, a plaintiff has to prove that the defendant has published (or is reponsible for the publication of) defamatory material that is reasonably understood to refer to plaintiff. Tort law protects a person's reputation from damage or injury by defamatory statements, of and concerning the plaintiff and published to a third-party or parties.
Tort liability can be imposed in many instances that include negligent behaviour towards a person or land, negatively affecting a person's reputation
or limiting freedom of movement. This module will aim to explain and take you through how and why liability can be imposed on a defendant, giving you and in-depth understanding of the nature of tortious liability.
There are many torts that will be discussed in this module. They include, for example, libel, slander, nuisance, negligence, trespass, assault and battery. Thus, it is not possible to provide one definition that encompasses all torts, considering how each tort has its own specific characteristics.
It is, therefore, best to think of the law of tort as the law of behaviour that is legally 'wrong' or 'tortious', giving rise to an entitlement to a remedy for the claimant.
Whilst it may not be possible to precisely define what tort is, various principles can be identified that help establish when a tortious liability arises. It has to be noted, however, that there is no predominance of any one principle. The principles that can be turned to are:
· Compensation
· Fault
· Retributive justice (punishment)

· Deterrence
· Economic efficiency
· Loss distribution

Tort law also aims to protect individual interests from a harm that is actual or threatened. However, not all interests are protected and some benefit from better protection than others. This is as a result of the importance of an interest reflected by society through the years. The interests protected include: Personal harm , harm to property ,harm to reputation ,harm to financial interests and harm to the due process of law.

(7) What are types of tort liabilities ?

There are a number of specific types of tort liabilities that form the basis of the majority of civil lawsuits in the United States. These include, among others: Negligence, intentional Infliction of emotional distress, assault, battery,trespass, products liability.

Tort law divides most specific torts into three general categories:

1.Intentional Torts – the causing of harm by an intentional act, such as intentionally conning someone out of his money.

2.Negligent Torts – the causing of harm through some negligent act, such as causing a car accident by running a red light.

3.Strict Liability Torts – the result of harm incurred due to the actions of another, with no finding of fault by the defendant.

The additional and separate specific torts include:

Defamation Torts, Nuisance Torts, Privacy Torts
and Economic Torts

(1) Intentional torts are acts committed with the intent to harm another, or to deliberately interfere with an individual's rights to bodily safety, emotional tranquility, privacy, control over property, freedom from deception, and freedom from confinement. Intentional torts commonly include such issues as assault and/or battery, false imprisonment, invasion of privacy, theft, property damage, fraud or other deception, and trespassing.

Intent is a key issue in proving an intentional tort, as the injured party, called the Plaintiff, must prove to the court that the other party, called the Respondent or Defendant, acted intentionally, and knew that his actions could cause harm. In some cases, the Plaintiff need only prove that the Defendant should have known that his actions could cause harm. Many intentional torts may also be charged as criminal offenses.

Intentional tort case examples:

Johnny stops by the local bar for a few drinks before he heads home after work. After drinking four cocktails, Raymond gets into his car, and runs a stop sign, crashing into another car, seriously injuring its occupants. Although Johnny might argue that he didn't know he would hurt someone, it is expected that Johnny should have known that driving under the influence is likely to cause harm, or to kill another person.Because Johnny intentionally drank alcohol, knowing he planned on driving home, and any reasonable person should know that drinking and driving could result in harm, he has committed an intentional tort. In addition, Johnny may be criminally charged with .

(2) Negligent Torts

The acts leading to claims of harm or injury in negligent torts are not intentional. There are three specific elements that must be satisfied in a claim of negligence:

1.The defendant must have a duty or owe a service to the plaintiff or victim
2.The defendant must have failed that duty, or violated a promise or obligation to the plaintiff
3.The plaintiff must have suffered an actual loss, injury, or damages that were directly caused by the plaintiff's actions, or failure to act

(3) Strict Liability Torts

Strict liability refers to the concept of imposing liability on a defendant, usually a manufacturer, without proving negligent fault, or intent to cause harm. The purpose of strict liability torts is to regulate activities that are acknowledged as being necessary and useful to society, but which pose an abnormally high risk of danger to the public.

Such activities may include transportation and storage of hazardous substances, blasting, and keeping certain wild animals in captivity.
The possibility of civil lawsuits under strict liability torts keeps individuals or corporations undertaking such dangerous acts diligent in
taking every possible precaution to keep the public safe.

(4) Suing Under Strict Liability Tort

In a strict liability lawsuit, the law assumes that the supplier or manufacturer of the product was aware the defect existed before the product
reached the consumer. Because of this, the plaintiff need only prove that harm or damages occurred, and that the defendant is responsible.
To successfully bring a civil lawsuit under a strict liability tort, the following

elements must be proven:

1.The named defendant is the manufacturer of the defective product.

2.The product was defective when the plaintiff purchased it.

3.The defect was present when the defendant sold the product.

4.The defect caused the plaintiff's injuries or damages.

5.The injuries or damages caused by the product's defect were reasonably foreseeable by the defendant.

A plaintiff in a strict liability lawsuit may be awarded additional damages if he can prove that the defendant knew about the defect when the product was sold to consumers.

Suing Under Strict Liability Tort case example:

Peter buys a new car from local Auto dealership. Only three months later, The car dealership noticed Peter brakes felt soft, so the car dealership took peter car to dealer's repair shop. They told peter just needed new brake pads, replaced them, and sent the auto car dealership on her way. A month later, while Peter was driving on a busy freeway, Peter brakes failed, and Peter crashed into another car. Peter's car was very badly damaged, and Peter suffered a broken arm and a concussion.

Peter discovers, while researching the brake problem Peter had been having with his car, that this particular model has had brake problems since it was first released for sale to the public. In digging deeper, The car dealer discovers that Zoom Auto knew the car's brake system was defective before they sold the cars, but determined it would be too expensive to bring them all back into the factory to change out the brake systems.

In suing Zoom Auto, The car dealer must use this information to prove:
1.Zoom Auto manufactured the defective vehicle.

2.The car's brake system was defective when she bought the car.

3.The car's brake system was defective when Zoom Auto sold the car to Peter.

4.The brake defect caused Peter's injuries, as well as the severe damage to her car.

5.It was reasonably foreseeable that selling a car with a defective brake system would cause injury to consumers.

6.Zoom Auto knew about the defective brake system in this particular model car before they sold the vehicles, yet chose to sell them anyway, in blatant disregard of the safety of consumers.

Under the Federal Tort Claims Act ("FTCA"), the U.S. government is liable for the tortious acts of individuals acting on the government's behalf, in the same way a private party would be liable in similar circumstances. The amount of damages that may be awarded in such a lawsuit, however, is limited, with no allowance for punitive damages, or interest accumulated prior to the date of judgment.

The FTCA specifies that anyone wishing to file a tort claim against the United States must do so, in writing to the appropriate federal agency, within two years of the date the tort occurred. This means that the statute of limitations on filing an administrative claim under the FTCA is two years.

Any individual wishing to file an administrative claim for reimbursement for damages or injury must demonstrate that:

1.His property was damaged, or he was injured, by the actions of an employee of the federal government.

2.The federal employee was acting in his official capacity at the time the damage or injury occurred.

3.The federal employee acted wrongfully, or negligently.

4.The federal employee's wrongful or negligent act caused the plaintiff's damages or injury.

In most tort cases, an individual who desires to file a claim under the FTCA must first file an administrative claim with the federal agency that employs the employee that caused the damages. This requires filling out the required forms, and providing documents or other evidence supporting the claimant's position. Forms and additional information can be obtained from the Department of Justice website.

Once an administrative claim has been filed, the agency has six months to respond to the claimant. If the claimant is not happy with the agency's response or decision, he has six months from the date the response was mailed to him to file a civil lawsuit under the FTCA. In the event the federal agency does not respond to the claimant within the six month time frame, the claimant may go ahead and file a civil lawsuit, but his six-month statute of limitations does not begin to run until the agency actually provides a response or decision. When filing a claim under the FTCA, the lawsuit must be filed in the U.S. District Court, which is the official name of the federal court, in the district where the tortious act occurred, or where the plaintiff lives.

(5) trespass and false imprisonment

Trespass

A trespass is an unauthorized action with respect to a person or property.
A trespass to the person consists of any contact with someone's person for which consent was not
given. This is technically described as a battery. An assault would be a situation where a plaintiff
reasonably believed a battery upon his person was about to be committed. An example of an assault
would be where one person swings his fist at another person. If the person made contact, this would be an assault and battery. A defense to assault and battery would be in cases of self-defense.

A trespass to land involves going on or above the property of another without permission. A
trespass can also involve the unpermitted use of the airspace of another's property as well as
actually going on the actual property. However, this rule has been modified to allow the flight of
aircraft above the land as long as it does not interfere with the proper use of the land.
A trespass to personal property is the use of someone's property without the person's permission.

A conversion occurs when personal property is taken by a defendant and kept from its true owner
without permission of the owner. Conversion is the civil side of the crime of theft. The concept is
based on the tortfeasor converting something to their own use. It also requires an intention to
deprive the true owner of their ownership – so if you put a mobile in your pocket thinking it was
yours it would not be conversion.

False Imprisonment

False imprisonment involves detaining a person without that person's consent. It can take the extreme form of kidnapping or the less extreme form of detaining a shopper for suspected
shoplifting without reasonable grounds.
A defense to false imprisonment would be consent of the detainee, or if a

store owner had

reasonable grounds to believe that the detainee was guilty of shoplifting (shopkeeper's privilege).

This privilege allows a store owner (or his employee) to detain a suspected shoplifter based on reasonable suspicion for a reasonable time.

A customer was shopping at the handbag counter of the defendant's store. She did not make any purchase and left the store. When she was a few feet outside the store, an employee of the store tapped her lightly on the shoulder to attract her attention and asked her if she had made any

purchase. When she inquired why, the employee asked, "What about that bag in your hand?" The

customer said that it belonged to her and she opened it to show by its contents that it was not a new bag. The employee gave the customer a "real dirty look" and went back into the store without

saying a word. The customer then sued the store for false imprisonment. Was the store liable? No.

Judgment would be for the store. There was no false imprisonment because there was no actual

detaining of the customer. The circumstances did not show the use of force or threat of force that

stopped the customer from proceeding on her way. Her action of stopping and showing the contents of her handbag was voluntary.

(6) negligence and malpractice

Negligence is a failure to follow the degree of care that would be followed by a reasonably prudent

person in order to avoid foreseeable harm. A person can be negligent if he or she acts with less care than a reasonable person would use under similar circumstances.

Bob drove a car on a country road at 35 miles an hour. The maximum speed limit was 45 miles an

hour. He struck and killed a cow that was crossing the road. The owner of the cow sued Bill for the

value of the cow. Bill said that since he was not driving above the speed limit, there could be no

liability for negligence. Was this defense valid? No. A person must at all times act in the manner in

which a reasonable person would act under the circumstances. The fact that Bill was driving within

the speed limit was only one of the circumstances to consider. The weather or the condition of the
road may have made it unreasonable to drive at 35 miles an hour. Driving slower than the speed
limit does not in and of itself prove that the driver was acting reasonably.

The reasonable person standard varies in accordance with the situation. The degree of care required of a person is that which an ordinarily prudent person would exercise under similar circumstances. This does not necessarily mean a degree of care that would have prevented the harm from occurring.

The elements required to establish negligence are: the presence of duty; a voluntary act or failure to act (an omission) that breaches the duty; proximate causation of harm; and damage (i.e., the breach of duty causes harm to the plaintiff).
Torts involve duties created by law. Just because someone is hurt does not mean that someone else
must pay for the harm. There must have been a duty which has been breached. A plaintiff will not
be allowed to recover from a defendant if the defendant did not breach a duty that was owed to the plaintiff. For example, if a burglar breaks into my house and trips over an item of furniture, I am not liable to the burglar because I had no duty to him. However, if a guest in my house trips over a piece of furniture, I may have a duty to that guest. The breach of duty must result from a voluntary act or failure to act.

In order for someone to be legally responsible for damage, it is necessary to show that the wrongful act was the proximate cause of the harm. The injury must be shown to be the natural and probable result or consequence of the alleged act of negligence. The plaintiff must prove that the defendant's negligence proximately caused the Plaintiff's injury. There may be more than one proximate cause of an accident.

The final element of negligence is damages. A plaintiff may recover monetary damages to
compensate the plaintiff for economic losses such as lost wages and medical expenses. A plaintiff
may also recover non-economic losses such as for pain and suffering. The former are claimed on a
normal accounting basis, and the latter are at the discretion of the judge.

(7) Malpractice
Malpractice is a failure by a physician or other professional to use the skill and care that other
members of their profession would use under similar circumstances. When an accountant, doctor, attorney, or some other professional contracts to perform services, there is a duty to exercise skill and care as is common within the community for persons performing similar services. Failure to fulfil that duty is malpractice.

(8) Nuisance
Nuisance is a civil wrong, consisting of anything wrongfully done or permitted that interferes with or annoys others in the enjoyment of their legal rights. It is anything that annoys or disturbs the free use of one's property or that renders its ordinary use or physical occupation uncomfortable.

A nuisance is anything that interferes with the rights of citizens, the enjoyment of their property, or their comfort. It is to be noted that an unreasonable interference with another person's use and enjoyment of his/her property is determined by the injury caused by the condition and is not determined by the conduct of the party creating the condition.

A nuisance is differentiated from a trespass to land. A trespass is an invasion of a person's interest in the exclusive possession of their land, whereas a nuisance is an interference with the use and enjoyment of the land and does not require interference with the possession. A person injured by a nuisance can recover damages in an action at law for tort. Similarly, damages can also be recovered for injury resulting from the legal use of a property, if such use substantially damages the property of another.

Nuisances are divided into different subheads such as nuisances per se, public or common nuisances, private nuisances, etc. A public nuisance exists when an act or condition is subversive of public order or constitutes an obstruction of public rights. In other words, a public nuisance involves an unreasonable interference with a right common to the general public. In order to constitute a public nuisance, it is not necessary that it affects the whole community. It is a public nuisance if the injury or annoyance affects the people of a local neighborhood. Public nuisances always arise out of unlawful acts.

Therefore, acts that are lawful or authorized by a valid statute, or which the public convenience demands, cannot be a public nuisance. A public nuisance can constitute either a crime or may be the subject of a civil action by public officials or private individuals. At common law, the term "public nuisance" covers a variety of minor criminal offenses that interfer, for example, with the public health, safety, morals, peace, or

convenience. Public nuisances include for example, a manufacturer who has polluted a stream and might be fined and be ordered to pay the cost of cleanup. Public safety nuisances include shooting fireworks in the streets or storing explosives.

A private nuisance is a civil wrong that affects a single individual or a definite number of persons in the enjoyment of some private right which is not common to the public. In other words, a private

nuisance is a substantial and unreasonable interference with the private use and enjoyment of one's land. Examples include interference with the physical condition of the land, disturbing the comfort of its occupants, or threatening injury or disturbance in the future.

Nuisances that interfere with the physical condition of the land include vibration or blasting that damages a house; destruction of crops; raising of a water table; or the pollution of soil, a stream, or an underground water supply. Examples of nuisances interfering with the comfort, convenience, or health of an occupant are foul odors, noxious gases, smoke, dust, loud noises, excessive light, or high temperatures, e.g. a landowner burning plastic and old tyres so that the smell and smoke affect his neighbours.

(9) Defamation

Defamation is the communication of a false statement that harms the reputation of an individual. The law of defamation protects a person's reputation and good name against communications that are false and derogatory. Defamation consists of two torts: libel and slander. Libel consists of any defamation that can be seen, most typically in writing. Slander is a form of defamation that consists of making false oral statements about a person which would damage that person's reputation. If I spread a rumor that my neighbor has been in jail and this is not true, I could be held liable for slander.

A person is liable for the defamation of another. In order to prove defamation, the plaintiff must prove:

● that a statement was made about the plaintiff's reputation, honesty or integrity that is not true;

• there was publication to a third party (i.e., another person hears or reads the statement); and

• the plaintiff suffers damage as a result of the statement.

Public figures have a more difficult time proving defamation. Politicians or celebrities are understood to take some risk in being in the public eye and many of them profit by their public persona. A celebrity must prove that the party defaming them knew the statements were false, made them with actual malice (intent to harm), or was negligent in saying or writing them. Proving these elements can be an uphill battle. However, an outrageously inaccurate statement that's harmful to one's career can be grounds for a successful defamation suit, even if the subject is famous. For example, some celebrities have won suits against tabloids for false statements regarding their ability to work, such as an inaccurate statement that the star had a drinking problem.

Another important aspect of defamation is the difference between fact and opinion. Statements made as "facts" are frequently actionable defamation. Statements of opinion or pure opinion are not actionable. Some jurisdictions decline to recognize any legal distinction between fact and opinion. To win damages in a libel case, the plaintiff must first show that the statements were "statements of fact or mixed statements of opinion and fact" and second that these statements were false.

Conversely, a typical defense to defamation is that the statements are opinion. One of the major tests to distinguish whether a statement is fact or opinion is whether the statement can be proved true or false in a court of law. If the statement can be proved true or false, then, on that basis, the case will be heard by a jury to determine whether it is true or false. For example, your statement of opinion is just an opinion, and does not contain specific facts that can be proved untrue. "The waiters and waitresses at the Tivoli Restaurant are too slow and the food is too spicy." This is a statement of opinion. "I got food poisoning at the Tivoli Restaurant" is potentially a defamatory statement if, in fact, the restaurant can prove that you never contracted food poison."

Some statements, while libelous or slanderous, are absolutely privileged in the sense that the statements can be made without fear of a lawsuit for slander. The best example is a statement made in a court of law. An untrue statement made by a witness about a person in court which damages that person's reputation will generally not be held to be liability to the witness as far as slander is concerned.

(10) Strict liability torts and Vicarious liability
    Strict Liability
Strict or absolute liability is the legal responsibility for damage or injury, even if the person found strictly liable was not at fault. In order to prove strict liability in tort, plaintiff needs to prove only that the tort happened and that the defendant was responsible for the act or omission.

In the case of strict liability in the USA, neither good faith nor the fact that the defendant took all possible precautions is a valid defense. A common example of strict liability is imposing product liability in the case of defectively manufactured products.

Strict liability applies especially in cases involving hazardous or dangerous activities.
Generally, liability based on a tort only arises where the defendant either intended to cause harm to the plaintiff or in situations where the defendant is negligent. However, in some areas, liability can arise even when there is no intention to cause harm or negligence. For example, when a contractor uses dynamite which causes debris to be thrown onto the land of another and damages a landowner's house, the landowner may recover damages from the contractor even if the contractor was not negligent and did not intend to cause any harm. Basically, society is saying that the activity is so dangerous to the public that there must be liability. However, society is not going so far as to outlaw the activity.

Example: Acme Construction Company was constructing a highway. It was necessary to blast rock with dynamite. The corporation's employees did this with the greatest of care. In spite of their
precautions, some flying fragments of rock damaged a neighboring house. The owner of the house sued the corporation for damages. The corporation raised the defense that the owner was suing for tort damages and that such damages could not be imposed because the corporation had been free from fault. Was this defense valid? No. While ordinarily fault is the basis of tort liability, there are cases in which absolute liability is imposed on the actor. This means that when harm is caused, it is no defense that none was intended or that due care had been exercised to prevent the harm.

Other examples of absolute liability situations would be harm caused by storage of flammable gas and explosives, factories which produce dangerous fumes or smoke in populated areas, and the production of nuclear material. Vicarious liability is the responsibility of the superior for the acts of their subordinate. It is the responsibility of a third party who has the right, ability or duty to control the activities of a violator.

Typically liability flows from the relationship of master and servant. The relationship includes the
power to direct the servant in the execution of the duties of his/her employment, and to control the
acts that no injury is done to third persons.
An employer can be held vicariously liable for an employee's tortious act against the person or
property of a third party in a transaction of the employer's business. If a negligent act is committed by an employee acting within the general scope of her or his employment, the employer will be held liable for damages. For example, if the driver of a gasoline delivery truck runs a red light on the way to a gas station and strikes another car, causing injury, the gasoline delivery company will be responsible for the damage if the driver is found to be negligent.

(9) Why do some countries feel need to reform
tort law?
For US government tort law system example, Some American citizen feels needs to reform tort law in US. I shall indicate reasons as below:

In US tort law system, the term tort reform has been bandied about as a hot-button issue since the congressional elections in 2010. The average American citizen does not understand what tort reform actually means, and has no idea that it has no bearing on any laws, but is a general acknowledgement that the amount of damages awarded to victorious plaintiffs in tort lawsuits has grown too large.

In past decades, juries have sought to sufficiently reimburse plaintiffs for tortious wrongs committed against them, as well as to punish many defendants for actions the jury considers. Many proposed tort reform acts have proven to be ill considered, however, as they seek to make it more difficult for people to file civil lawsuits, to make it more difficult for plaintiffs to obtain a jury trial on a civil matter, and to cap the amount of money plaintiffs can be awarded in various types of civil lawsuits.

While some people consider awards made to certain victorious plaintiffs, the truth is, some of these plaintiffs experience seriously increased costs of living, medical expenses, loss of income, and loss of quality of life, due to the tortious behaviors of others. An award of damages in the millions of dollars range may sound like a large award, but when considering it spread over the plaintiff's lifetime, it is often merely enough to get by.

● Mc Donald's tort negligent wrongdoing behavior to compensate big compensation sue amount case:

Tort reform has come under public awareness, as many people find publicized awards in civil lawsuits to be shockingly large. One of the most famous tort lawsuits in recent history in the case of a 79-year old woman who sued McDonald's restaurants when she spilled her coffee, and was burned.

Liebeck v. McDonald's Restaurants sue compensation case:

In 1992, 79-year old Stella Liebeck spilled a cup of McDonald's coffee in her lap, sustaining third degree burns to both legs. The severity of the full-thickness burns required skin grafts. This involved stripping skin from other areas of Liebeck's body to graft onto the burned areas which were no longer able to grow skin on their own, leaving her with even more wounds to heal.

When McDonald's denied Liebeck's request to pay her medical bills, she filed a civil lawsuit.

During the course of the case, it was discovered McDonald's had received hundreds of other complaints from customers complaining that their coffee had caused severe burns, and that the corporation's operations manual specified the coffee was to be kept at 180-190 degrees Fahrenheit. It is known and accepted, by the scientific and medical communities, that liquid at that temperature, if spilled onto a person, causes third degree burns in three to seven seconds.

A jury awarded Liebeck $200,000 in compensatory damages to pay for medical bills and other related expenses. Because it was clear the company knew its coffee was kept at a dangerously high temperature, and was therefore likely cause serious injury, the jury also awarded Liebeck $2.7 million in punitive damages, which amounted to the company's sales revenue from just two days of coffee sales.

While many proponents of tort reform view this case as a supreme example of a frivolous lawsuit with a shockingly high award, the truth is, McDonald's knew its coffee could cause third degree burns, yet continued

to specifically instruct its restaurant employees to keep and serve
it at that temperature. Ms. Liebeck's injuries were severe, her painful third
degree burns requiring skin grafts. McDonald's was given an opportunity to
settle the matter out of court, but they refused to do so.

To judge this case relates whether McDonald ought need to compensate
to the old woman or not? It depends on these related Legal Terms and Issues
as these factors below:

Civil Lawsuit – A lawsuit brought about in court when one person claims
to have suffered a loss due to the actions of another person.

Criminal Offense – An act committed by an individual that is in violation
of the law, or that poses a threat to the public.

Damages – A monetary award in compensation for a financial loss, loss
of or damage to personal or real property, or an injury.

Defendant – A party against whom a lawsuit has been filed in civil court,
or who has been accused of, or charged with, a crime or offense.

Entity – An individual, company, association, trust, or other
organization that is legally recognized in the eyes of the law. A legal entity
is able to enter into contracts, take on obligations, pay debts, be sued, and
be held responsible for its actions.

Personal Property – Any item that is moveable and not fixed to real
property.

Plaintiff – A person who brings a legal action against another person or
entity, such as in a civil lawsuit, or criminal proceedings.

Punitive Damages – Money awarded to the injured party above and
beyond their actual damages. Punitive damages, also referred to as
"exemplary
damages," are ordered for the purpose of punishing the wrongdoer for
outrageous misconduct in a civil matter.

Real Property – Land and property attached or fixed directly to the land,
including buildings and structures.

Ultimately, the judge reduced the amount awarded by the jury to
$640,000, and the case was appealed by McDonald's, which finally settled
for
an undisclosed amount before the appeal concluded. In this case, the
current tort system worked property, as it prompted McDonald's to settle
the case, quite possibly because of a concern that the award would be
boosted back up to the original amount awarded by the jury. However, the
final result. McDonald does not need to compensate to this old woman

when she sues the accident compensation. The severity of
the full-thickness burns required skin grafts. This involved stripping skin
from other areas of Liebeck's body to graft onto the burned areas
which were no longer able to grow skin on their own, leaving her with even
more wounds to heal.

In conclusion, due to the compensation is too much, so it is unreasonable compensation amout to sue McDonald needs to pay to this old woman client's body hurt claim. However, US court still need McDonald to compensate part body hurt loss to this old woman client's accident claim for her stripping skin from other areas of Liebeck's body to graft onto the burned areas which were no longer able to grow skin on their own, leaving her with even more wounds to heal. So, it explains why US tort law needs to be reformed again, such as this compensation amout is too much and unfair and unreasonable to this McDonald's accident body hurt to this old woman client's case.

● Why is tort reform necessary in the United States?

Tort reform is necessary in the US because insurance companies, big business, big pharma
and big medical interests, and unscrupulous irresponsible entities and persons need the protection of the courts and laws so they can make more obscene profits and face little or no risk when they cause harm to people through their negligence and intentional acts that a jury determines are reasonably forseeable
to cause harm. And do not believe a jury acts without restraint. The trial judge can dismiss cases before they get to the jury or set aside unsupportable jury verdicts. Appeals courts can also reverse trial results that are
unreasonable. Hence, big business is now spending many millions of dollars getting judges they support elected to the highest courts in the various states, where their pro-big business interests can be furthered. Years ago, these state judge races were not fueled by such enormous funding.

Many tort reform promoters want our laws to abandon its position in protecting the people from harm intentionally or negligently caused by others. Lets limit the damages these wrongdoers can be accessed. Lets limit legal fees and damage awards on medical malpractice and elder care neglect cases so lawyers will not be able to accept all but the most extreme cases of wrongdoing. Alot of people think they support tort reform until it is their parent or child or themselves who suffered injury due to someones wanton

or reckless act. Some of these reform supporters bought into the idea of lower insurance insurance
premiums or lower medical costs promised in return for tort reform laws passed. I suggest they were sold a lie.

Of course, tort reform is necessary in the US because the Constitutional right of people to seek redress of wrongs against them in the courts, including their constitutional rights to a jury, equal protection under the law, and so many protections you can find in our Constitution and Bill of Rights, hinder business profits and cost big pharma too much money to properly warn people of the dangerous side effects of their drugs, they knew about. Is not progress and profit more important than corporate accountability?

● The Absolute Need for Tort Reform

I'm planning on looking at various problems liberals whine and complain about needing more government and show how each and everyone one of those problems is caused in multiple ways by more government. And I already know that in in most of the cases it's going to come back to Tort Reform being needed, so I figured I should put together some evidence for it.

Tort Reform? Tort law is the law that governs civil lawsuits. Right now the Democratic Party (and quite a few RINOs) as a wholly owned subsidiary of the American Bar Association
(read unethical scum and ambulance chasers) are against tort reform (probably because it would be good for the nation).

However reforms like limiting the amounts you can receive for pain and suffering, limiting lawsuits to negligence or the but-for test (where you can sue unless you can prove but for the plaintiff's actions the defendant would be fine), creating a loser pays system (where the loser has to pay the winner's legal fees), penalties for ambulance chasers who bring in one frivolous lawsuit after another, and more power for judges to throw out frivolous cases. Simple things like that.

This may all sound silly, or even pointless. But take a look at the warning labels on items when you buy them. Almost all of these are because stupid people used these items in an inappropriate way...and then they sued. And when the company they sued loses the costs hurt you either by raised prices or fewer employees being hired.

Even when the company doesn't win, they've still lost because of legal fees. And you still bear the burden of the cost. All because stupid people also happen to be litigious people (also because lawyers tend to be somewhere on the evolutionary chain below pond scum).

Every state that has engaged in tort reform has seen lower costs, more employment, fewer court costs and more efficient courts, a stimulated economy and more tax revenue. They've even seen fewer deaths because doctors aren't afraid anymore to actually practice medicine.

Tort reform is primarily a state by state issue, and you should see where your state is in terms of tort laws and if you have time try and get tort reform in your state. However there are also a few federal issues (as there are federal civil cases) and thus we need some federal reform as well. But don't believe me. Here is a body of op-eds, reports, studies and opinions by people who have done far more research than I.
It all comes to the same conclusion, we need tort reform.

1. Most cases aren't civil lawsuits so this isn't a problem.

That's because most companies will settle because they know juries are unreliable and composed of 12 people too dumb to get out of jury duty. Thus most things that come under the law governed by tort law are handled out of court.

2. Evil corporations want tort reform.

Any time the whole argument is against corporations, you know it's a BS argument. Corporations can be good or bad depending on their behavior. Corporations will actually behave better when only legitimate lawsuits are brought against them and we don't knee jerk dismiss every lawsuit as the work of an ambulance chaser.

3. Tort reform limits people from receiving their right to a jury trial. Juries are one of the most basic defenses of a democracy.

First we live in a republic, a system designed on the premise that people are fickle and can be stupid. And for anyone who wants to plead the intelligence of juries I have two letters for you: OJ. Juries are a last ditch effort that no one wants, it's why so many criminal cases are plead out, and so many civil suits dealt with out of court. Juries are at best unpredictable and at worst consistently illogical . They're trying to make a pointless emotional argument that has nothing to do with facts.

4. Tort reform will limit the amount that people have a right to when they are harmed by people and corporations.

The only thing I know we want to limit is "pain and suffering" costs. If you're a professional athlete and have your body injured by a corporation you could still sue them for loss of income for millions. But that doesn't

often happen. It's pain and suffering judgments
that create the most in awards and it's these that are often the most
ridiculous.

5. Injured people will not be able to file suit if we have tort reform.

Actually since there will be fewer frivolous lawsuits from ambulance chasers throwing everything against a wall to see what sticks, people with real cases (but who don't have sleazy lawyers who know how to work the field) will have a better chance of getting their case heard.

(10) What is the tort law system difference between US and UK ?

In U.S. tort legal system, U.S. tort law is based primarily on common law—in which judicial rules are developed on a case-by-case basis by trial judges—rather than on legislation. Tort liability is assigned using two basic standards: strict liability and negligence. Under strict liability, injurers are held fully liable for their victims' losses without regard for whether they were actually negligent or intended to harm anyone.

Under a negligence standard, by contrast, injurers are held liable only if they failed to meet a certain standard of care. According to legal scholars, a number of important developments have increased the scope of liability for torts in the United States.

Otherwise, in UK legal system, early English tort law, the antecedent of U.S. tort law, was chiefly concerned with making injurers pay for the losses of their victims, with little emphasis
on fault or negligence. That standard was used in the United States until the 19th century, when U.S. common law established negligence as the basis for tort liability. However, strict liability continued to apply in certain cases, such as injuries caused by wild animals kept as pets or damage to crops caused by trespass of domestic animals.3 Some scholars argue that the requirement for plaintiffs to show that defendants had been negligent effectively limited the scope of the U.S. tort system.

The 20th century saw public policy increasingly emphasize victim compensation and accident reduction. The enactment of workers' compensation laws— which established a public insurance system aimed at lowering employers' payments while making workers' recovery of damages automatic—played an important role in the evolution of tort law and policy. Before workers' compensation programs, the only remedy that injured workers had was to prove their employers negligent through the tort system. Workers favored legislation instead because they often had been unable to recover damages or had experienced delays or high costs when they had been successful. For their part, employers favored legislation because it limited their liability and made payments predictable.That shift away from tort law to a public compensation system led to more thought about how tort liability could be improved or better applied in other types of cases.

By the 1940s, legal scholars had begun to think about two ways in which the tort system could serve the wider goal of enhancing social welfare. First, they saw the economic concept of "cost internalization" as a tool for reducing accident rates: if potential injurers know they will be held liable for accidents, they will take appropriate action to avoid liability. In that view, by awarding damages to compensate victims, tort law would serve as a mechanism to ensure that potential injurers faced the appropriate future costs of their actions. Second, some scholars argued that the tort system could provide a kind of accident insurance for victims. They did not focus on the possibility that an expanded liability system could increase carelessness on the part of potential victims, nor did they adopt any of the methods that traditional insurance policies use to deal with that problem. Rather, they focused exclusively on the distributional goal of relieving victims of the burden of accident losses and spreading that burden across a broader population.

For UK legal system practice was product liability. Historically, product liability was dealt with either as a breach of warranty under contract law or as a tort subject to the negligence standard. Under contract law, recovery in such cases was limited to repair and replacement of the product; under tort law, recovery was limited by the difficulty of proving negligence. It is different to US product liability act.

In the 1960s, the courts moved rapidly toward a standard of strict liability for defective products; in 1964, that standard was accepted and recommended by the American Law Institute in its second Restatement of the Law volume

on torts. By the mid-1970s, most states had adopted provisions that were either identical or similar to those in the Restatement.

What is a tort to UK ?

The law of tort is wide-ranging body of rights, obligations and remedies applied by the courts in civil proceedings.

It provides remedies relief for those who have suffered loss or harm following the wrongful or negligent acts of others.

A tort is a civil wrong by the 'tortfeasor' that unfairly results in loss or harm to another. This makes the tortfeasor liable to the other. Tort is distinguishable from two other kinds of law – criminal law and contract law, and is dealt with by the civil courts.

Unlike tort, the criminal law are wrongs against society and is comprised in legislation and prosecuted by the authorities, and dealt with in the criminal courts. In contract law, the rights and obligations between the contractual parties are governed by the contract itself and not by the law of tort.

However, sometimes the line is blurred between tort, crime and contract law. For instance, violent offences against the person such as assault and battery can be prosecuted by the Crown; and a damages claim can also be brought in the civil courts by the victim.

● Parties to an action in tort

Anyone can sue in tort if they suffered harm or loss as a result of someone else's civil wrong. There is the potential for children to sue, including children who are born with disabilities due to harm inflicted prior to birth; and even a husband and wife can sue each other.

Claimants can sue a wide range of tortfeasor. The following are examples of different types of individuals and other parties who can potentially face an action against them under the law of tort:

· Individuals
· The Crown
· Companies
· Employers
· Employees
· Independent contractors
· Occupiers of premises
· Individuals who have caused damage to another's reputation
· Dangerous drivers
· Individuals in the medical profession
· Occupiers of recreational premises

What are the elements of the Law of Tort?

Negligence

Whilst there are different types of tort, negligence is by far the most common tort for which claimants take legal action.

There are four elements to the tort of negligence. Each of these must be present for a claim to be successful:

1.The negligent party owed a duty of care to the victim.

2.There was a breach of the duty of care.

3.Causation (the negligent caused the injury/loss).

4.Damage or injury occurred.

What is England law elements of Tort of Negligence ?

Negligence simply refers to failure to use reasonable care. In common law negligence is explained as the action taken that

contradicts with what an ordinary reasonable member from a given community would act in that same community. It's doping something that a prudent person wouldn't do. It is the legal cause of damage if it directly, naturally and continuously contributes in causing that damage. It is thus taken that were it not for negligence, then the damage

would not have occurred. On the other hand, a tort is any wrongful act except breach of trust or contract resulting in injury to another individual's property and reputation for which the injured individual qualifies to be compensated.

There are three elements in the tort of negligence; duty of care, breach of the duty and damages. Duty of care means that any single person must always take reasonable care so that he can avoid omissions and acts that he can foresee reasonably as likely to result to injury to his neighbor. In negligence law, a neighbor is that person who is directly and closely affected by one's act such that one is supposed to have him/her in contemplation to be affected when directing the mind to the omissions and acts in question. Standard of care must be proved by deciding whether the defendant in question owed the plaintiff a standard of care, the level of standard of care that the defendant owed the plaintiff and lastly, by determining whether another reasonable person in the same field like the defendant would do the same.

Breaching of the standard of care must be proved by checking how likely the injury was and how it can be regarded, injury gravity (whether the plaintiff at all engaged in a dangerous activity) and efforts that may be required in order to remove injury risk (whether the defendant failed to act reasonably). Damages caused by the defendant must have resulted through the breach of duty of care and that this was not remote.

(11) What is the difference between tort and contract ?

The difference between tort and contract is easy to identify if you understand the concept of each clearly. In fact, the terms Tort and Contract are not uncommon or ambiguous terms. Indeed, we have heard their use occasionally and thus have a fair idea as to what they mean. However, in order to understand the difference between tort and contract, we must first pay attention to the definitions of each term separately.

The concept of Tort is an important subject in civil law. Indeed, civil courts hear and determine many cases involving Torts. The term Tort is derived from the Latin word 'Tortus,' which is translated to mean "wrong" or "civil wrong." It is similar to the concept of a crime in that it involves some form of wrongdoing inflicted on another person. However, unlike a crime, a Tort is more personal. Thus, while a crime constitutes a wrongful act caused not only to a person but to the entire society as a whole, a Tort constitutes a wrongful act caused only to a person. It is thus a private wrong. Torts typically encompass wrongful acts in the form of harm or injury caused to a person or their property. The party that has suffered harm or injury will file a civil action in court against the person who inflicted the harm. If the court finds that a Tort has been committed, the court will typically order the defendant to pay compensation or provide other relief to the injured party. This compensation is generally known as the remedy of Damages.

Examples of Torts include occupier's liability, nuisance, economic Torts, negligence, defamation, or product liability. The Tort of negligence revolves around the concept of the duty of care owed by one person to another. Failure to exercise this duty of care to another in certain situations will result in the Tort of negligence. An example of such an instance is when a person drives recklessly and causes harm to a pedestrian.

Torts are categorized into Intentional Torts (a person had substantial knowledge that his/her actions would result in harm),strict Liability Torts (Torts which focus only on the physical aspect of the wrongful act), and Negligent Torts. When a person commits a Tort, the court will not look at the Tort but at the harm or injury suffered by the victim as a result of that Tort. Keep in mind that breach of contract does not fall within the definition of a Tort.

● Difference Between Tort and Contract

A tort is a wrong that is personal in nature.

A Contract is a familiar concept to all of us. In simple terms, it refers to an agreement between two or more parties, which is enforceable by law. Formally, however, it is defined as an agreement between two or more parties, who intend to create legal obligations, to perform some work or service. Contracts may be oral or written, although today it is most often in written form. The defining feature of a Contract is that it is not just an agreement to perform some work or service, but that work or service is typically performed in return for a valuable consideration. Thus, consideration is a vital element in a Contract.

Consideration is usually in the form of a payment. In addition to Consideration, a Contract must typically contain several other elements in order to be valid and recognised as a Contract in law. Thus, there must be an offer and an acceptance of that offer, the parties must have capacity to contract, and the subject matter of the Contract must be legal. Contracts may take various forms such as Unilateral Contracts or Bilateral Contracts. Like in the case of a Tort, a breach of one or more of the terms of the Contract or the entire contract itself may result in the remedy of Damages been awarded. Thus, contract is a agreement between two or more parties that is enforceable by law and the difference between Tort and Contract is simple: a Tort constitutes a civil wrong while a Contract refers to an agreement between two or more parties.

In conclusion, the principle difference is between tort and contract. It may include as below:

· A Tort refers to a civil wrong. It is a private wrong in that it constitutes a wrongful act in the form of a harm or injury caused to a person or their property. Torts are categorized into Intentional Torts, Strict Liability Torts, and Negligent Torts.

· A Contract refers to an oral or written agreement between two or more parties, who intend to create legal obligations, to perform some work or service in return for a valuable consideration, which is usually in the form of a payment.

● What is the concept of Tort and Contract difference?

When a person commits a Tort, the court will not look at the Tort but at the harm or injury suffered by the victim as a result of that Tort. The court will typically order the defendant to pay compensation or provide other relief to the injured party. An examples of Torts include occupier's liability, nuisance, economic Torts, negligence, defamation or product liability.

A Contract has an offer and an acceptance of that offer and the parties involved must have capacity to contract. A breach of Contract by either party may result in awarding the remedy of Damages. An example of a Contract is an agreement between Company A to provide a security service to Company B in return for a valuable consideration paid by Company B to Company A.

(12) What is the difference between a tort and a criminal act?

When it comes to the difference between a tort and a criminal act, the two can be especially difficult to distinguish. Here are the basics:

· Legally speaking, a tort occurs when one's negligence directly causes damage to a person or property.

· A crime is defined as a wrongdoing against society.

● Tort law means

Tort law is the area that determines whether or not a person should be held legally responsible for someone' injuries or damaged property. This area of law also governs the types of damages an injured person is able to collect, such as medical expenses or lost wages. Tort disputes are settled in civil court settings with one party seeking compensation from another.

There are several types of torts, and each covers a wide array of cases. They include:

· Negligence. Negligence is the most common type of tort. These take place when a person acts without due care and, as a result, unintentionally injures someone.

· Strict Liability. In strict cases (for example, animal attacks or defective products) one party is always held liable regardless of circumstances – even if the injury was caused unintentionally.

· Intentional Torts. Intentional torts occur when an individual intentionally causes harm to another, such as battery or defamation. Confusingly, intentional torts often involve criminal activity and are therefore often confused with criminal wrongdoing. However, if the injured party chooses to sue for compensation, the case then also becomes a tort case.

● What are mean of Crimes law?

Crimes are different from torts in that those who have committed a crime have acted against society rather than just an individual person. Crimes are actions that a state or the federal government has deemed illegal.

● Can Crimes Also Be Torts?

As mentioned above, crimes can also be torts in some cases. For example, let's say Logan and Chris find themselves arguing. Logan punches Chris angrily and breaks Chris's nose as

a result. Logan is then accused of battery – a criminal charge – because it is illegal to physically assault another person in such a way. However, Chris also decides to sue Logan for the medical costs he has accrued due to his broken nose. As soon as Chris sues for his own personal damages, the case also becomes a tort. Logan may have to repay his debts to both society (in the criminal case) and Chris (in the tort case).

● Workers Compensation on contract law protection

When You're Injured
 · How to File a Work Injury Claim
 · Reporting a Work-Related Injury or Condition
 · Workers' Compensation Overview

Obtaining Treatment & Benefits
 · Workers' Compensation for Law Enforcement Officers
 · Reasons Why Temporary Disability Benefits Can Be Terminated in Your Workers' compensation Case
 · Workers' Compensation Case Timeline
    Differences between Crimes and Torts

A crime is a wrong arising from a violation of a public duty. A tort is a wrong arising from the

violation of a private duty. Again, however, a crime can also constitute a tort. For example, assault is

a tort, but it is also a crime. A person who is assaulted may bring criminal charges against the

assailant and may also sue the assailant for damages under tort law. An employee's theft of his employer's property that was entrusted to the employee constitutes the crime of embezzlement as well as the tort of conversion. The police may prosecute a crime, and the offender is imprisoned, but this does not compensate the injured party; to obtain compensation the injured party will need to bring a claim in tort law.

(13) What does Economic torts mean?

Economic torts are defined as torts that have inflicted pure financial loss on someone. A primary example of an economic tort is 'passing off' in the course of business, whereby an individual or business attempts to pass off their goods as the goods of another – relying on the substantial goodwill associated with the original product or goods. A claim can be made for damages to compensate for the economic loss suffered.

Other claims in tort include tortious claims also include nuisance, occupiers liability, defamation, trespass and breach of confidence.

Remedies in tort,there are two key remedies available for claimants:

· Damages

· Injunction

What do Damages mean?

Damages provides financial compensation to the claimant for their losses. Damages can be broken down into the following subcategories:

· Nominal: where a tort has been committed but the victim has suffered no loss.

· Contemptuous: where the claimant is successful but the court considers that it should not have been brought and was without merit.

A very small or derisory amount of damages may be ordered in such cases.

· General: to compensate for non economic damages such as pain and suffering and emotional distress.

· Special: the claimant must plead these damages as part of the action and prove that the damage was in fact suffered. For instance, damage to property and medical expenses.

· Aggravated damages: if the court decides that the tort was committed in a malicious manner, ie. to harm the claimant's character or question his dignity, then aggravated damages may be awarded.

· Exemplary or punitive damages: these may be awarded when the court finds that the action committed by the defendant is so serious that an example needs to be made of them.

Injunctions means that in some cases, it may be appropriate to apply to the court for an injunction. An injunction is a court order prohibiting or requiring a certain course of action to be taken. This can be in addition to a damages claim.

What do defences to tort actions mean?

The following are defences to tort actions:

· Vicarious liability

· Contributory negligence

· Volenti non fit injuria

Vicarious liability means that where a tort was committed by an employee while undertaking his or her duties of employment, i.e. there was a close and direct connection with the harmful act committed by the employee and what they were employed to do, the employee can deny liability and claim that the employer was vicariously liable.

Contributory negligence means that this is a partial defence used whereby the claimant is accused of acting in a careless manner at the relevant time, and therefore contributed to the injuries or loss which they have suffered.

(14) Reasons need tort law ?

A tort is any civil wrong for which the law provides a remedy. Torts provide compensation for injuries to persons and property caused by the fault of another. There have always been concerns about whether there should be restrictions on tort law because of disagreements about who should bear the financial burden for an injury and what injuries should be compensable. Powerful lobbies of doctors, hospitals, insurance companies and product manufacturers are always appealing to Legislatures to limit the ability of the public to obtain compensation for violations of tort law. Consumers who are injured by defective products, victims of sexual harassment, drunk drivers, and many other civil wrongs are always under attack with their legal ability to be compensated for their injuries.

The purpose of tort law is to restore someone who has been injured as a result of the wrong of another to the condition they were prior to the injury by awarding them monetary damages which will pay for medical expenses, lost wages and compensate for physical and mental pain and suffering as a result of their injuries.

Beyond this, however, is the role that tort law plays in punishing the misconduct of corporations and individuals who cause harm to others through negligent misconduct. The existence of our tort law makes it more expensive for corporations and other potential defendants to be negligent or have negligent policies. The fear of being in a lawsuit and having a jury determine what damages have been incurred by a negligent corporation or individual, causes those potential defendants to be more careful and to have policies to prevent injury.

Without tort law, a corporation or individual may chose not to be more careful particularly when being careful requires the expenditure of money. Trial lawyers pursuing tort claims often uncover documents and cover-ups that can have deadly consequences to unprotected individuals.
Lawyers who handle cases involving personal injury do so on a contingent fee basis meaning they charge a percentage of recovery rather than an hourly fee which enables individuals with lesser incomes to bring suit against the most powerful individuals and corporations.

● Why the Tort System is Important ?

The tort system gives average people a way to influence powerful businesses and institutions and
change their dangerous practices and policies.

· For years, people reported instances of clergy abuse to church officials. However, it was not until
lawsuits were filed that church hierarchies began to institute procedures to punish offenders and
protect parishioners.

· As a result of lawsuits brought by patients' families, nursing home policies and procedures have been changed to better protect elderly patients.

· After individuals successfully sued companies, many re-designed their products, improved warnings,and in some cases, withdrew dangerous products from the marketplace. The tort system deters companies from putting profits ahead of safety.

· The prospect of paying damages provides the financial incentive for companies to ensure safety and refrain from harmful conduct, thereby preventing injuries in the first place.

· Corporate Risk Managers have reported that the threat of tort liability helps them motivate companies to improve product safety.

· Liability concerns have helped spur the manufacture of safer consumer products, such as flame retardant pajamas and cars with rear-seat shoulder belts and improved fuel tank design.

The tort system helps limit the government's role.

· Without the tort system to police and deter business misconduct, government probably would have to assume a greater role in protecting the public from negligent and unscrupulous business conduct.

(15) Tort law sample cases question

Architect and engineering firm owed duties of care to Provincial to exercise due diligence in their work on project contract liability in tort case:

To satisfy the court that compensation should be made, the plaintiff in a tort action must substantiate that:

1. the defendant owed the plaintiff a duty of care,

2. the defendant breached that duty by his or her conduct, and

3. the defendant's conduct caused the injury to the plaintiff.

Both the architect and engineering firm owed duties of care to Provincial to exercise due diligence in their work on the project.

The architect breached his contractually-owed duty of care by ignoring the engineer's recommendation and not doing a detailed enough soils test for building construction. The engineering firm breached its implicit engineering duty of care by submitting a soils report based on inadequate data. The combination of these actions indeed caused financial injury to Provincial. These combined mean that both the engineering firm and the architect satisfy the requirements for tort liability and so should be required to compensate

Provincial for any damages that resulted as concurrent tortfeasors.

(Optional: Mention a specific case.) This case is very similar to the 1979 decision by British Columbia Court of Appeal: Corporation of District of Surrey v. Carrol-Hatch et al.: An architect designed a police station which was built and later required extensive structural changes due to soil problems. Engineers working for the architect recommended doing deep soil tests, but the architect rejected the request. The engineers then submitted a soils report to the owner based on two shallow soil tests. Result: engineers 40% liable, architect 60% liable to the owner for structural changes. As such, the result for this case will likely be similar.

Principles of tort law,

"To satisfy the court that compensation should be made, the plaintiff in a tort action must substantiate that:

1. the defendant owed the plaintiff a duty of care,

2. the defendant breached that duty by his or her conduct, and

3. the defendant's conduct caused the injury to the plaintiff."

The standard of care engineers have a duty to uphold is "to use reasonable care and skill of engineers of ordinary experience."

In this case, dependent on the terms and conditions of the contract, CRUDDI may or may not be liable to OILI for the costs of replacing the air conditioning unit and perhaps even lost production as a result. If this is the case, then CRUDDI could take action against MESSI for an amount equal to the damages; otherwise, OILI could commense action against MESSI directly.

MESSI will likely be found liable under tort for the air conditioning replacement and lost productivity as a result of the original unit's inadequacy because

1) they as engineers had a duty to "use reasonable care and skill of engineers of ordinary experience" in designing the air conditioning unit,

2) they breached this duty by designing a wholly inadequate system for the purpose it was intended, and

3) this breach caused financial injury to OILI .

Answer to this contract law case

Yes, I do think the owner would be successful in a tort claim against the engineer.For liability in tort to exist, three things must be present

1. "the defendant owed the plaintiff a duty of care,

2. the defendant breached that duty by his or her conduct, and

3. the defendant's conduct caused the injury to the plaintiff."

In fact, this is an actual case (Law Text section 4.4): 1983 by Ontario Supreme Court: Unit Farm Concrete Products Ltd. v. Eckerlea Acres Ltd. et al.; Canama Contracting Ltd. v. Huffman et al.

Contractor engaged by owner to construct barn to be placed over a manure pit.

The contractor succeeded with action against an engineer of the dept. of Agriculture, because the contractor relied on advice of the engineer, a friend of the contractor, in confirming that his (ultimately very faulty) design was sufficient. Interestingly, the engineer was not a consulting engineer, nor was he employed to review the plans; he just gave them a quick look as a friend and told the contractor "Good set of plans. I like the detail. Wish I could spend that amount of time on each project. Keep up the good work." The engineer didn't know he was being consulted, but the court pointed out that,

when "being held to account for negligence, it is not what we subjectively feel or think but what our conduct objectively makes the other person believe we feel or think." Each found 50% responsible for damages.Contractor appealed this case to the Court of Appeals, which held the engineer 75% responsible and the contractor 25% responsible.

As such, the result in this case will be the same due to precedent. For liability in tort to exist, three things must be present .

1. "the defendant owed the plaintiff a duty of care,

2. the defendant breached that duty by his or her conduct, and

3. the defendant's conduct caused the injury to the plaintiff."

In this case, SPECS owed ACE a duty of care to design a procedure which conformed with the standard practice at the time, simply by virtue of being engineers, but also by virtue of their contractual relationship. Phil Scooper had a similar duty to KING through contract to act according to the generally accepted practice of his trade, and KING had a duty through contract to ensure that services they hire as part

of their contract with ACE are carried out correctly. Both parties breached their duties by their conduct, and the combination of these breaches caused extra costs and a four-week delay to ACE. As such, Phil Scooper and SPECS are concurrent tortfeasors to ACE (although Scooper

is technically a tortfeasor to KING and KING to ACE), and likely will be found liable to compensate ACE for the direct extra costs and the indirect ones associated with a four-week delay.

QUEEN will likely be found vicariously liable for Scooper in line with the fundamental principle of tort law being "to compensate victims" and not "to punish the negligent."

Principles of tort law:

1. the defendant owed the plaintiff a duty of care,

2. the defendant breached that duty by his or her conduct, and

3. the defendant's conduct caused the injury to the plaintiff.

In this case, the new engineer owed Mammoth a duty of care owed by all engineers, but specifically in his capacity as advisor on the matter of whether or not to use the substitute fill material. The new engineer acted negligently by approving a material as safe without doing the necessary analysis to determine whether it was so; breaching a duty of care. Finally,

this conduct caused financial injury to Mammoth. As such, Mammoth is entitled to claim damages necessary to replace the material and cover any costs
incurred by the associated delay from the engineering firm (or perhaps its insurance company). The firm (or insurance company) would be vicariously liable for the new engineer in line with the fact that the fundamental principle of tort law is to compensate the victims,brather than punish the negligent.

For liability in tort, the three requirements are:
1. "the defendant owed the plaintiff a duty of care,
2. the defendant breached that duty by his or her conduct, and
3. the defendant's conduct caused the injury to the plaintiff."

In this case, the engineering firm (specifically, the recent engineering graduate who designed the sprinkler system and the P.Eng who reviewed it) owed National a duty of care. In not familiarizing him/herself with the NFPA codes at least to the point of determining the sprinkler coverage limits, the engineering graduate breached this duty of care, UNLESS he/she specifically pointed out to the P.Eng his/her only very brief review of the NFPA. Certainly though, the P.Eng breached his/her duty of care in only briefly reviewing the work of the recent engineering graduate and finding it satisfactory.

Finally, this combination of the conduct by the engineering graduate and the P.Eng caused substantially more fire damage to the plaintiff than would have been caused had they not acted negligently (as was substantiated by the consulting engineer's expert opinion "the fire should have been quickly extinguished and would not have spread to any great extent").

According to the Regulations under The Professional Engineers Act of Ontario, negligence is "an act or omission in the carrying out of the work of a practitioner that constitutes a failure to maintain the standards that a reasonable and prudent practitioner would maintain in the circumstances." This is exactly what the engineering graduate did (though ignorantly) in designing the sprinkler system, and also what the P.Eng did in finding the design satisfactory.

Certainly, given the satisfaction of the requirements of tort law, National will be compensated for all excess fire damage and the funds necessary to repair the faulty sprinkler system design. The question remaining is "from whom should this compensation originate?" The necessary principle of tort law to answer

this question is "The fundamental purpose of tort law is to compensate victims of torts."

Though perhaps the most directly at fault in this case, the recent engineering graduate is likely not in a good financial position to compensate National, and so will not likely be assigned liability.

The essential principles of tort law are;

(a) a duty of care,

(b) a breach of that duty,

(c) resulting damage, excess costs or injury as a result of the breach.

The architect had an overall duty of care to ensure a satisfactory system and the mechanical engineering firm to ensure design calculations were correct. These duties were breached and dollars were required to replace the air conditioning system. The engineering firm is vicariously liable with the employee

engineer who prepared the design and made significant errors. The engineering firm and the architect are jointly liable i.e. concurrent tortfeasors.

The failure occurred within two years which is within the limitation period for a claim in tort.

The total excess costs to meet completion must be sustained by the architect and the mechanical engineering firm. These costs include the $2,000,000.00 to complete the project and also the costs of delays to the developer/ owner. A likely outcome of the matter is the mechanical firm would be 70% responsible and the architect 30% responsible.

The liabilities of the soils experts Acme Underground, are to see the work is finished so payment by the municipality is limited to the original amount agreed. Since the extra cost is $350,000.00, then this is the basic liability. Other costs, e.g. fees of Subsurface Wizards would also fall to Acme. If the possibility of these liabilities were not included in the various contracts, it would be a suit in tort. A tort case has three elements:

a) a duty of care,

b) a breach of that duty,

c) resulting damages or excess costs to an injured party.

In this case, the soils experts, Acme Underground (a) failed to exercise the care that could reasonably be expected of competent practitioners and (b) made significant errors. The municipality is entitled to a contribution/

retribution for the (c) unplanned difficulty. Assuming there is no privity of contract between the owner and the soils experts, the suit would be in tort, unless the engineer's contracts enable action on behalf of the owner.

The likely outcome is all excess costs would be assessed to Acme Underground, an amount of $350,000.00. Sharp did extra work as well which he might claim against Acme.

Even though the municipality's budget was $1,800,000.00 and there was a resultant total cost of $1,650,000.00 plus $350,000.00, the municipality should still only pay the contract price of $1,650,000.00.

Principles of tort law:
"To satisfy the court that compensation should be made, the plaintiff in a tort action must substantiate that:
1. the defendant owed the plaintiff a duty of care,
2. the defendant breached that duty by his or her conduct, and
3. the defendant's conduct caused the injury to the plaintiff."

In this case, the architect breached his contractually-owed duty of care by ignoring the engineer's recommendation and not doing a detailed enough soils test for building construction. The engineering firm breached its implicit engineering duty of care by submitting a soils report based on inadequate data. The combination of these actions indeed caused financial injury to Provincial: as such, the architect and engineer could be found concurrent tortfeasors.

(16) What Are The 4 Elements Of Tort Law?

Every civil lawsuit except for contractual disputes falls under the category of tort law. Essentially, any civil lawsuit is tort law.
The premise behind these laws is to provide compensation to victims of wrongdoings. However, not every tort case is successful.
So how can you make sure your tort case is successful? For any civil lawsuit to be successful, there need to be four elements of tort law present and proven in court. In this post, we'll outline the four elements of tort law. After reading this post, you'll know where you stand in any potential
tort lawsuit case.

A duty of care must always be present in any tort law claim if it's to be successful. This is basically stating that there is a duty of
care on part of the person or the manufacturer of some product that must

be upheld. For example, drivers of cars have a duty of care to drive safely and not intoxicated or under the influence of drugs.

Going with the example above, let's say you have Brian who can legally drive in the UK and has his own car. Well, Brian has a certain duty of care that he must adhere to at all times as a responsible driver and not engage in behaviours that could endanger others. Examples of this duty of care he has are not getting behind the wheel drunk or affected by drugs. This is a duty of care Brian has that is enforceable by law so he must adhere to it at all times.

● Breaching Duty Of Care

We've established in the previous section that Brian has a certain duty of care and legal responsibility he must adhere to.

If he were to breach this care, whether it's intentional or unintentional, he could be liable for a tort. For example, if he was to drive his car drunk and then run a red light, which resulted in an accident then he would be found guilty of breaching his duty of care. Therefore, he'd be liable for a tort.

● Causation Which Results In Suffering

This part is crucial for a tort case because there needs to be the action that has caused suffering to the victim. In the absence of the cause, there is no case for a tort.

A key aspect of causation that a court will explore is whether or not the victim's injuries would have occurred had the offender not committed the specific action that resulted in the injury to the victim.

Let's return to the case of Brian being drunk and running a red light. If while running a red light, he crashed into another car,which resulted in the other driver becoming permanently brain damaged from the crash, then this would be sufficient causation for a tort.

● Damage Or Injury to above case?

It is difficult to decide damage or injury to this case, because without the damage or injury sustained then there is no basis for a tort lawsuit.

Let's roll with the case of Brian above. The other driver he crashed into must have sustained some sort of injury from his negligent actions.

If there is an absence of physical, mental, or emotional damage then Brian cannot be liable for a tort.

It's also important that these damages are proven for there to be a legitimate case. To prove mental and emotional damages, you'd need to get expert proof from professionals in this area. To prove physical damages, advice from medical professionals would be required.

What Happens If A Tort Is Proved ?

If all the four elements of tort law above are present then a tort has been committed. In this circumstance, there is going to be a court
case where either damages or an injunction occurs. There are various damages that can be awarded in this instance such as full compensation where the victim must be fully compensated monetarily for his/her suffering.

However, there are various subcategories of damages that can be awarded like nominal damages, special damages, aggravated damages, and more. Victims will pursue any of the damages most applicable to their specific situation in order to get the compensation they deserve. Ultimately, it's up to the court to decide what damages will be awarded.

What does negligence mean in tort law ?

Negligence refers to failure to use reasonable care. In common law negligence is explained as the action taken that contradicts with what an ordinary reasonable member from a given community would act in that same community. It's doping something that a prudent person wouldn't do. It is the legal cause of damage if it directly, naturally and continuously contributes in causing that damage.

It is thus taken that were it not for negligence, then the damage would not have occurred. On the other hand, a tort is any wrongful act except breach of trust or contract resulting in injury to another individual's property and reputation for which the injured individual qualifies to be compensated. There are three elements in the tort of negligence; duty of care, breach of the duty and damages.

Duty of care means that any single person must always take reasonable care so that he can avoid omissions and acts that he can foresee reasonably as likely to result to injury to his neighbor. In negligence law, a neighbor is that person who is directly and closely affected by one's act such that one is supposed to have him/her in contemplation to be affected when directing the mind to the omissions and acts in question. Standard of care must be proved by deciding whether the defendant in question owed the plaintiff a standard of care, the level of standard of care that the defendant owed the plaintiff and lastly, by determining whether another reasonable person in the same field like the defendant would do the same. Breaching of the standard of care must be proved by checking how likely the injury was and how it can be regarded, injury gravity (whether the plaintiff at all engaged in a dangerous activity) and efforts that may be required in order to remove injury risk (whether the defendant failed to act reasonably).

Damages caused by the defendant must have resulted through the breach of duty of care and that this was not remote.

For hospital doctor's a duty of care to patient case example:

In this case in question, B (patient) was examined by A (doctor) since he had a chest problem. A had asked B all the relevant questions just like any other doctor in this field would have done. But after being discharged B died due to a heart attack. It is the prescription that B's wife believes caused the death of her husband. Applying the tort of negligence,

B who is the claimant in this case must satisfy three elements as required by the clinical negligence law. A owed B a duty of care since he is a medical professional. In order for the court to rule in the favor of B (claimant), she must show that A breached the duty of care owed to her husband by treating him negligently. This should include a sound proof that A did not establish a reasonable standard of skill and care. This would call for detailed medical evidence in our case. In the end, a loss/damage (death) caused must be shown that its causative agent was due to A's breach of duty.

For manufacturer's duty of care to consumer case example:

Taking as an example, Donoghue v Stevenson is a case where the tort of negligence developed. It was in 1929 when Donoghue (plaintiff) bought a ginger beer manufactured by Stevenson (defendant). This ginger beer was in an opaque bottle that could not allow one to see its contents clearly. Donoghue consumed some of the beer but as she poured the remaining beer into her glass, decomposed remains of a snail

were seen in the glass. She had gastro-enteritis and nervous shock which she claimed were due to the snail remains in the beer. Just like in our case of A and B, the defendant (Stevenson) owes a duty of care to the plaintiff (Donoghue). The main issue in deciding this case was on establishing whether Stevenson owed Donoghue a duty of care. Lord Atkin said decisively that Donoghue had to show that the damages

caused to her were due to the breach of duty owed to her by Stevenson in taking reasonable care to avoid it. The court by using previous cases like Heaven vs. Pender asserted that negligence comes due to a moral wrongdoing where the offender is obliged to pay.

Additionally, a person must take reasonable care to escape all acts and omissions that one can reasonably foresee that they can injure ones neighbor. They thus ruled that this may be a grave law defect where consumers cannot sue manufacturers for negligently mixing a drink with poison. By stating that the manufacturer must have the foreseeability of the effects on actions taken on the neighbors (consumers).

In case of A and B, it shows that there is medication negligence according to UK law.
The defendant after examining the plaintiff and asking all the relevant questions, he did not fully exercise his duty of care.

The medication that killed B can only be taken as lack of exercising the required standard of care for a professional of A's caliber. A doctor in the same position would have been expected to give medications to B that coincided with the problem that he had. According to UK law, medical negligence occurs where an individual who is trained in the medical profession fails to fulfill his duties of care to his patients in a standard manner.

B's wife must that have to proof just like it was proved in above case by the court whether there is duty of care owed to her husband by A.
A doctor has to take all the actions towards his patients to ensure that whatever he does will not cause any injury to them. Comprehensive medical evidence is required here to show that B died because of medication negligence of A. This may be hard for her to proof since the heart attack may have been caused by other health problems. Three pre-conditions formulated in Caparo v Dickman for imposition of duty of
care (sufficient proximity between parties, it should be just, fair, and reasonable in imposing the duty of care in the circumstances and foreseeabilty of harm) must come into play in A vs. B so that B can claim compensation. It's evident that sufficient proximity between A and B exists.

The prescription given to B may however not make A to foresee any harm because all the questions he asked and the examinations he carried out on B had convinced him that he was supposed to give B that prescription. However, despite this, a doctor is supposed to act just like all others would do in the same profession. It is the duty of A to exercise standard of care after examining B and asking all the questions to make sure that diagnoses is not performed to the detriment of the patient (B).

For Tort of negligence of auditor case example:

Tort of negligence is also applied in Caparo v Dickman (1990) HL. In this case, the auditors of the company had prepared the accounts that however could not show that the company had been making losses. On seeing the accounts of the company, Caparo thought that since this company was not making any losses as per the auditors' accounts, it was advisable for him to buy shares in the same company. This company was however making losses. Caparo (plaintiff) thus alleged that it was through negligence that he was owed a duty of care.

A previous case, Sutherland Shire Council v Heyman (1995) was referred to and it was declared that the law must come up with novel categories in negligence in accordance with the already established categories. It was rejected for extension of duty of care to indefinable people or class of persons who are owed. In this case, it was ruled that there was no duty of care owed.

The auditors won this case since there was no case that could hold them to have a duty of care to the plaintiff.

To the auditors, establishing whether there was a duty of care required the court to determine whether the loss to the plaintiff was foreseeable.

This was not possible for the auditors. Again, there was no established proximity between the two parties to the case. Thus it was not just, fair or even reasonable for imposition of duty of care.

In Perrett v Collins (1998) CA, a plane built by Collins crashed and Perrett, a passenger was injured. This was a light aircraft that had been severally inspected at various stages. After its completion, Mr. Usherwood who was one of the inspectors approved it. Authorities had given certification that the plane was airworthy. This shows that both the inspector and the certifying authority were liable due to negligence

as they had certified this experimental plane fit to be flown. The duty of care was thus to be extended to any passenger in it. The public is supposed to be protected from any injury through mindful operation of the plane system. A passenger in such a plane has to be compensated

as this is negligent operation. By doing this, they have imposed a duty of care that is owed to the public by Collins.

For a duty of case to doctor and injuries patient case example:

Duty of care was also established in Watson v BBBC (1999) CA (Goodey, 2007). The defendant, British Boxing Board of Control could not provide sufficient medication. Watson, a boxer suffered brain damage as he was injured on the ring. Evidence provided showed that those brain injuries would have been prevented if there was better medication at ringside. Here, the sports body owed all participants a duty of care. Injury in boxing competitions is always foreseeable. Proximity was also created by the licensing system.

By looking at all the circumstances it was fair, reasonable and just in imposing duty of care. Duty of care alleged was not avoiding to cause personal injury but to have reasonable care that ensures that injuries caused are properly treated. These two cases seem to concur with the case of A and B. By being a doctor who is professionally trained; it means that A is a registered doctor who is expected to perform his duties just like other doctors in the profession. He owes a duty of care to all his patients. By being a registered doctor, it establishes proximity between A and B. Drugs administered to a patient are not guaranteed that they will always produce the expected results. Injury is thus foreseeable. Looking at all the circumstances in A vs. B, it was fair, just and reasonable to impose a duty of care. These two cases helps us to use the three pre-conditions of establishing that a duty of care exists as alleged by B's wife.

A doctor must exercise a standard duty of care to his patients. B's wife is claiming that her husband died due to the faulty medication that was given. After asking questions and examining B, A gave medical treatment that B's wife thinks was the cause of her husband's death. A in his profession is supposed to carry out his activities just like others would in the same field. His actions were supposed to be reasonable. It's all irrelevant for the defendant to claim that the medical treatment he gave B was the right one. His perception or what he thinks was okay is irrelevant since expectations are; he must act reasonably. It doesn't matter here if A considers his conduct fine; the standard is what would be expected of a reasonable person in medical profession. Standard of care in negligence doesn't result to absolute duty in prevention of injury.

Duty instead amounts to what the reasonable person is supposed to do to prevent injury from occurring. Reasonable test would be used here so that it can be decided what would be the reasonable behavior of A. In this case, the court would consider several factors. Special characteristics of A (defendant), special characteristics of B (claimant), how far it was practical to prevent this risk and magnitude of this risk. For A, he is a doctor and thus he has special skills (profession). Law expects a doctor to exhibit competency standards just like another doctor would do. This amounts to reasonable behavior. This same standard would apply even if the defendant was inexperienced or experienced.

For negligent act to learner driver and driver teacher case example:

In Nettleship v. Weston (1971), it was ruled that a learner driver was judged against standards of competent driver. Weston's inexperience could not be used as an excuse that her driving was below expected standard from a competent driver. Weston was thus considered negligent

as her negligent act resulted in damage. In the case of A vs. B, A would be held negligent as he has acted below the expected competence level. When considering the claimant (B), the court would have expected A (reasonable person) to look into incapacity or special characteristics which would have increased the injury. Magnitude of the risk would also be considered. This incorporates chance of the damage occurring and then the seriousness of the resultant damage. This may be illustrated in Vaughan vs. Menlove case where Vaughan built a haystack while Menlove who was a neighbor occupied a cottage that was near this haystack. Vaughan was given advice that his haystack could catch fire as it was not properly ventilated. It later caught fire. It was ruled that a reasonable person could have taken the necessary precautions.

The court in the case of A v B will thus consider how far it was practical to prevent the risk. In medical negligence, it is stated that a doctor cannot be held negligent in cases where he provides proof that what his

did is an act that has been agreed by the relevant body in the medical profession. A doctor can defend compensation to the claimant successfully if he shows that the reputable body of doctors would act in the same way as he did. In A v B, A had asked B all the relevant questions which another doctor in the same position would have done. Additionally, A had examined B properly

as he was complaining of chest pains. It clearly shows that medical treatment or prescription was given to B after doing all what any other reputable doctor would have done. It's clear that A as a medical expert had an opinion that was reasonable. The medication that he gave B was after weighing up the benefits and the risks involved. It's through this that he made his logical conclusion to give that particular treatment. This is just like in the case of Bolam v Friern Hospital Management Committee 1957.

In this case, a patient was treated for psychiatric problems yet he had an electric shock. The relaxant drugs administered led to broken bones. In the profession, there were doctors who felt that these drugs are not supposed to be given while others felt that they should. Since some doctors believed that these drugs administration was okay, the court ruled in favor of the doctor as this was a practice

that was in accordance with other professionals.

For doctor's duty of care to patient case example:

Another example is Bolitho vs. Hackney Health Authority 1997 where a two year old was admitted to hospital with breathing difficulties but was not seen by the doctor. He alter died of a heart attack. His mother claimed that he should have been seen by a doctor and incubated but failure to this resulted to his death. An expert witness from the doctor was produced which showed that incubation would

not have been the correct treatment for Bolitho while the claimant (Bolitho's mother) also came with a witness who said that incubation would have been the best treatment. Here the court ruled in favor of the doctor by stating that the opinion of the medical experts was reasonable and they had weighed up the risks and benefits.

Their conclusion was thus logical. It was thus declared that the doctor was negligent. The same case would apply in A vs. B. A has the capacity to produce evidence that all the examinations that he did and the questions asked were the relevant things any medical expert would have used. A thus weighed the risks, benefits and had a logical conclusion when he gave that particular medication to B. A was not liable for breach or it's totally possible to declare that there was breach of duty.

Death occurred in this case. B's wife must however prove that death was caused by breach of duty. The omission/negligence of A must be shown to be the cause the death of B. The UK law does not make defendants liable and infinitum. Instead, tests are applied to determine

what injury was caused by the defendant. The major test that would be applied here is 'but for' test. It simply means that the court will ask itself whether the claimant would not have suffered the injury 'but for' the omission/negligence by the defendant. There is no exact connection between the death of B since his death through a heart attack could have been due to other health problems. B's wife must in addition prove that the death caused was not remote from A's breach. A would only be liable for those injuries he would have caused B and he could have reasonably foreseen them at breach time.

The law of neglience claimant to succeed, the court must be satisfied that the defendant in question owed him a duty of care, that there was breach of duty by the defendant and finally the claimant's damages were as a result of the breach. Thus in our case, its well established that A as a doctor owed B a duty of care, but breach of the doctors duty could not be established

though death (damage/injury) occurred. Since all the elements in tort law are not served, then B's wife does not have a sufficient legal standing to take this case to court.

(16)Difference Between Tort Law and Criminal Law

We know that they both involve an act of wrongdoing. Tort means wrong. A crime, on the other hand, also denotes a wrong, a very serious one. Despite the fact that both recognise and declare certain acts as wrongful and therefore unacceptable, there is a difference. It lies in the types of wrongful acts that fall within the purview of each body of law.

What is Tort Law?

A Tort refers to a civil wrong. This means that Tort Law is dealt with in a civil proceeding. Tort Law encompasses situations in which harm has been caused to a person or property. Typically, the person who suffered harm initiates an action in a civil court against the person who caused the harm. Further, in a case involving Tort Law, the person who suffered injury sues the party at faul to in order to obtain relief or compensation for the injury. Compensation under Tort Law is typically awarded in the form of damages. Damages can include damages for loss of earnings, property, pain or suffering, financial or medical expenses.

Think of Tort Law a party seeks compensation of a financial nature for the loss he/she suffered. Examples of Torts include negligence, defamation, liability for defects in products, nuisance or economic torts. Negligence revolves around the duty of care and the failure to exercise a duty of care in a particular instance; for example, causing a motor accident.

It has three categories of Torts: Intentional torts, such as when a person had fair knowledge that his/her action would cause the harm, strict liability torts, which by their very definition exclude the degree of care exercised by the guilty party and instead focus solely on the physical aspect of the action such as the harm caused. There are also negligent torts, which involve the unreasonableness of a guilty party's actions.

What is Criminal Law?

Criminal Law encompasses the world of crime. It is defined as a wrong arising from the violation of a public duty. Think of Criminal Law as dealing with wrongful acts that affect society or the public collectively; in the sense that it disrupts the peace and order of society. This is in contrast to Tort Law, which deals specifically with wrongful acts that affect an individual personally.

Criminal Law is a body of law that regulates the conduct of society and ensures the protection of citizens by punishing those who do not act in accordance with such law. The crimes of murder, arson, rape, robbery and burglary are crimes that affect the society as a whole. For example, if there are a series of murders committed by one person, more commonly referred to as serial killing, then, the safety of society is at risk. Crimes falling within the purview of Criminal Law are dealt with in a criminal proceeding. Criminal law deals with instances in which an individual commits a crime against societal rules. For example, robbing a bank is considered criminal activity. Civil law, on the other hand, takes over when a dispute exists between private individuals. Case in point, one major area of civil law involves divorce and other family law proceedings.

In some cases, an individual may choose to sue another for injuries or damages. This is called tort law, and it falls under the umbrella of civil law. Although tort law is considered part of "civil law," many other areas of civil law exist as well. These include divorce and family law, contract disputes, wills and property disputes. Any dispute between private individuals, as stated above, typically fall under civil law jurisdiction.

Tort law is the largest area of civil law. The purpose of tort law is to determine whether or not an individual should be held legally accountable for the injury of another person. Tort law is also used to determine whether or not an individual should be compensated for his or her injuries and how much money is owed. For example, if someone slips and falls in a workplace accident, tort law is responsible for determining if the employer is liable for the individual's injuries and the amount of workers' compensation due.

3 Types of Tort

There are three prominent areas of tort law:

•Intentional tort. An intentional tort is when an individual purposefully engages in conduct that causes an injury or damages. For example, defamation and fraud each fall under intentional tort.

•Negligence. Negligence takes place when one person fails to do their duty to prevent injury or accident, leading to damages. Negligence includes slip and falls and car accidents. It's the most common type of tort.

•Strict liability. Sometimes absolute liability applies to a tort case. This occurs when one party is solely responsible for damages or injury. These include cases of defective products and animal attacks.

When compared to tort law, penalties are more severe in criminal law. Though tort law aims at providing compensation to the victim; punitive damages are also awarded in special cases. Almost all jurisdictions have enacted laws for protecting the citizens from wrongdoings, which are classified as crimes and torts. Both criminal law and tort law are intended to punish the offenders and deter others in society from indulging in such wrongdoings. If both crimes and torts are wrongful acts that are against the interests of society, then why are they treated differently? In fact, crimes and torts are different in various ways. In order to find out the difference between torts and crimes, you have to understand their meanings.

Every person has a legal duty to respect others' legal right and not to infringe such rights. Defamation is an example of a tort in which the reputation of a person is damaged by another. So, tort is a private wrong that affects the person or property of an individual. It is a civil wrong for which the aggrieved party may sue the wrongdoer for damages, according to tort law. A crime is an action or omission that constitutes an offense that may be prosecuted by the state and is punishable by law. It is a wrongful act committed in violation of a law prohibiting it, or omitted in violation of a law ordering it. In short, certain acts are classified by the state as crimes, and committing such acts gives rise to criminal liability. Robbery is an example of a crime. So, a crime is a public wrong, which is considered as a wrongdoing against society as a whole. It is a criminal wrong, for which the wrongdoer is punished by the state, according to criminal law. Given below is a comparison of torts and crimes, and the laws regarding these wrongdoings.

In concluson, both criminal law and tort law are used for taking corrective action against wrongdoers. As torts are wrongdoings against individuals, tort law is aimed at providing redress to aggrieved parties and deterring people from committing torts. The main purpose is to compensate the victim for the harm he/she suffered as well as crimes are considered as wrongdoings against the state or society as a whole. Certain acts are classified by the state as crimes, and such acts are forbidden by law; as they threaten public safety and welfare. Though a crime may have created an immediate victim(s), the state is considered as the ultimate victim; because a criminal (like a robber) can be dangerous for any person in society if he is let loose. So, the main purpose of criminal law is to protect society from crimes.Civil law is any law that is not criminal. Tort law is a subset of that — the law of non-criminal interpersonal injury (personal or economic). It does not include such civil issues as probate, family, civil rights, property law, or bankruptcy, among others.

CHAPTER TWO

Crime Law

(1) Criminal Law definition

A body of rules and statutes that defines conduct prohibited by the government because it threatens and harms public safety and welfare and that establishes punishment to be imposed for the commission of such acts. The term criminal law generally refers to substantive criminal laws. Substantive criminal laws define crimes and may establish punishments. In contrast, Criminal Procedure describes the process through which the criminal laws are enforced. For example, the law prohibiting murder is a substantive criminal law. The manner in which government enforces this substantive law—through the gathering of evidence and prosecution—is generally considered a procedural matter.

Crimes are usually categorized on their nature and the maximum punishment that can be imposed. It involves serious misconduct that is punishable by death or by imprisonment for more than one year. Most state criminal laws subdivide into different classes with varying degrees of punishment. Crimes that do not amount to violations. It is misconduct for which the law prescribes punishment of no more than one year in prison. Lesser offenses, such as traffic and parking infractions, are often called violations and are considered a part of criminal law.

Congress has the power to define and punish crimes whenever it is necessary and proper to do so, in order to accomplish and safeguard the goals of government and of society in general. State legislatures have the exclusive and inherent power to pass a law prohibiting and punishing any act, provided that the law does not contravene the provisions of the U.S. or state constitution. When classifying conduct as criminal, state legislatures must ensure that the classification bears some reasonable relation to the welfare and safety of society. Municipalities may make designated behavior illegal insofar as the power to do so has been delegated to them by the state legislature.

Laws passed by Congress or a state must define crimes with certainty. A citizen and the courts must have a clear understanding of a criminal law's requirements and prohibitions. The elements of a criminal law must be stated explicitly, and the statute must embody some reasonably discoverable standards of guilt. If the language of a statute does not plainly show what the legislature intended to prohibit and punish.

In deciding whether a statute is sufficiently certain and plain, the court must evaluate it from the standpoint of a person of ordinary intelligence who might be subject to its terms. A statute that fails to give such a person fair notice that the particular conduct is forbidden is indefinite and therefore void. Courts will not hold a person criminally responsible for conduct that could not reasonably be understood to be illegal.

A criminal statute does not lapse by failure of authorities to prosecute violations of it. If a statute is expressly repealed by the legislature, but some of its provisions are at the same time re-enacted, the re-enacted provisions continue in force without interruption. If a penal statute is repealed without a saving clause, which would provide that the statute continues in effect for crimes that were committed prior to its repeal, violations committed prior to its repeal cannot be prosecuted or punished after its repeal.

The same principles govern pending criminal proceedings. The punishment that is provided under a repealed statute without a saving clause cannot be enforced, nor can the proceeding be prosecuted further, even if the accused pleads guilty. A court cannot inflict punishment under a statute that no longer exists. If a relevant statute is repealed while an appeal of a conviction is pending, the conviction must be set aside if there is no saving clause. However, once a final judgment of conviction is handed down on appeal, a subsequent repeal of the statute upon which the conviction is based does not require reversal of the judgment.

Generally, two elements are required in order to find a person guilty of a crime: an overt criminal act and criminal intent. The requirement of an Overt Act is fulfilled when the defendant purposely, knowingly, or recklessly does something prohibited by law. An act is purposeful when a person holds a conscious objective to engage in certain conduct or to cause a particular result. To act knowingly means to do so voluntarily and deliberately, and not owing to mistake or some other innocent reason. An act is reckless when a person knows of an unjustifiable risk and consciously disregards it.

Ordinarily, a person cannot be convicted of a crime unless he or she is aware of all the facts that make his or her conduct criminal. However, if a person fails to be aware of a substantial and unjustifiable risk, an act or omission involving that risk may constitute negligent conduct that leads to criminal charges. Negligence gives rise to criminal charges only if the defendant took a very unreasonable risk by acting or failing to act.

(2) What does criminal intent mean?

Criminal intent must be formed before the act, and it must unite with the act. It need not exist for any given length of time before the act; the intent and the act can be as instantaneous as simultaneous or successive thoughts. A jury may be permitted to infer criminal intent from facts that would lead a reasonable person to believe that it existed. For example, the intent to commit Burglary may be inferred from the accused's possession of tools for picking locks.

Criminal intent may also be presumed from the commission of the act. For example, the intent to commit murder may be demonstrated by the particular voluntary movement that caused the death, such as the pointing and shooting of a firearm. A defendant may rebut this presumption by introducing evidence showing a lack of criminal intent. In the preceding example, if the murder defendant reasonably believed that the firearm was actually a toy, evidence showing that belief might rebut the presumption that death was intended.

Proof of general criminal intent is required for the conviction of most crimes. The intent element is usually fulfilled if the defendant was generally aware that he or she was very likely committing a crime. This means that the prosecution need not prove that the defendant was aware of all of the elements constituting the crime. For example, in a prosecution for the possession of more than a certain amount of a controlled substance, it is not necessary to prove that the defendant knew the precise quantity. Other examples of general-intent crimes are Battery, rape, Kidnapping, and False Imprisonment.

Some crimes require a Specific Intent. Where specific intent is an element of a crime, it must be proved by the prosecution as an independent fact. For example, Robbery is the taking of property from another's presence by force or threat of force. The intent element is fulfilled only by evidence showing that the defendant specifically intended to steal the property. Unlike general intent, specific intent may not be inferred from the commission of the unlawful act. Examples of specific-intent crimes are solicitation, attempt, conspiracy, first-degree premeditated murder, assault, robbery, burglary, forgery, false pretense.

Most criminal laws require that the specified crime be committed with knowledge of the act's criminality and with criminal intent. However, some statutes make an act criminal regardless of intent. When a statute is silent as to intent, knowledge of criminality and criminal intent need not be proved. Such statutes are called Strict Liability laws. Examples are laws forbidding the sale of alcohol to minors, and Statutory Rape laws.

The doctrine of transferred intent is another nuance of criminal intent. Transferred intent occurs where one intends the harm that is actually caused, but the injury occurs to a different victim or object. To illustrate, the law allows prosecution where the defendant intends to burn one house but actually burns another instead. The concept of transferred intent applies to Homicide, battery.

For murder criminal behavior example. It is not necessary to prove that the defendant intended to kill the victim. For example, a death resulting from arson will give rise to a murder charge even though the defendant intentionally set the structure on fire without intending to kill a human being. Furthermore, the underlying crime need not have been the direct cause of the death. In the arson example, the victim need not die of burns; a fatal heart attack will trigger a charge of felony murder. In most jurisdictions, a death resulting from first-degree murder, usually include arson, robbery, burglary, rape, and kidnapping.

(3) What does malice criminal behavior mean?

Malice is a state of mind that compels a person to deliberately cause unjustifiable injury to another person. At Common Law, murder was the unlawful killing of one human being by another with malice aforethought, or a predetermination to kill without legal justification or excuse. Most jurisdictions have omitted malice from statutes, in favor of less-nebulous terms to describe intent, such as purpose and knowing.

Criminal law has retained malice as an element in criminal prosecutions. malice is an essential element of first- and second-degree murder. According to the Supreme Judicial Court of malice is a mental state that "includes any unexcused intent to kill, to do grievous bodily harm, or to do an act creating a plain and strong likelihood that death or grievous harm will follow.

(4) What does criminal law motives mean?

Motives are the causes or reasons that induce a person to form the intent to commit a crime. They are not the same as intent. Rather, they explains why the person acted to violate the law. For example, knowledge that one will receive insurance funds upon the death of another may be a motive for murder, and sudden financial difficulty may be motive for burglary.

Proof of a motive is not required for the conviction of a crime. The existence of a motive is immaterial to the matter of guilt when that guilt is clearly established. However, when guilt is not clearly established, the presence of a motive might help to establish it. If a prosecution is based entirely on Circumstantial Evidence, the presence of a motive might be persuasive in establishing guilt; likewise, the absence of a motive might support a finding of innocence.

(5) What does Defenses mean?

Defenses Negating Criminal Capacity To be held responsible for a crime, a person must understand the nature and consequences of his or her unlawful conduct. Under certain circumstances, a person who commits a crime lacks the legal capacity to be held responsible for the act.Examples of legal incapacity are infancy, incompetence, and intoxication.

In legal view point, children are not criminally responsible for their actions until they are old enough to understand the difference between right and wrong and the nature of their actions. Children under the age of seven are conclusively presumed to lack the capacity to commit a crime. Between the ages of seven and 14, children are presumed to be incapable of committing a crime. However, this presumption is not conclusive; it can be rebutted by the prosecution through the admission of evidence that the child knew that what he or she was doing was wrong. Anyone over the age of 14 is presumed to be capable of committing a crime, but this presumption can be rebutted by proof of either mental or physical incapacity. So, children do not need to defence to responsible for a crime behavior in criminal view point.

(6) What does a criminal lawyer do?

Criminal lawyer needs to advises clients about the potential consequences of a course of action.
A criminal lawyer helps their client understand criminal laws. They also

help the client understand how their actions may or may not violate a criminal law. A defense attorney might help their client understand whether a proposed course of action is a crime. An attorney for the state might help law enforcement officers understand best practices for enforcing the law.

A criminal lawyer also need to help their client present their case or present a defense. A prosecutor or district attorney presents evidence and pursues prosecution of cases on behalf of the unit of government that they represent. They make decisions about whether to extend a plea offer. They present the evidence on behalf of the state at trial. A defense attorney helps their client present a defense. A defense attorney gathers evidence for their client. They evaluate the case in order to determine viable defenses. If they need to file pretrial motions, they make sure they file the motions in the right way.

In any countries, citizens have constitutional rights. No unit of government can pass a law that violates a person's right to be free from an unreasonable search and seizure. Law enforcement also can't keep a person in jail for an indefinite period of time. Criminal attorneys must know how the constitution and criminal law intersect. They must be aware of constitutional implications of law as they go about their work and advocate for their clients as necessary in order to protect and defend their constitutional rights.

Why does criminal lawyer need tp practise criminal law ?

A criminal law practice requires diverse skills and a capacity for memorization. It's also exciting. For lawyers who like frequent court appearances and the occasional appearance on television, criminal law is a good fit. Criminal lawyers must be comfortable in high pressure situations. They also must be able to think on their feet. There often isn't time to look something up or seek a second opinion when they must act in a matter of seconds to move to admit evidence or make an objection.

Criminal law is a good fit for lawyers who choose to focus on state laws in a small geographic region can expect to have multiple court hearings a week. They can expect to conduct trials and other contested hearings. Lawyers who focus on crime also have the academic challenge of building a case. They review police reports and interview witnesses. They examine possible defenses and determine whether or not they apply to the case. Being an effective criminal lawyer requires a well rounded mix of academic skills and oral advocacy. Criminal lawyers also benefit from having a high capacity for rote memorization. A criminal lawyer needs have good writing and speaking skill. Criminal lawyers can't rely on speaking or writing alone. A criminal lawyer must write clearly in order to properly file motions and help the court understand nuanced issues of law. They must also have the trial advocacy skills to conduct complex trials. Whether a lawyer advocates on behalf of the state or for an accused, they must also have the interpersonal skills to interact with the other side and the jury.

(7) What are stages in a criminal law case ?

In first stage, a criminal case starts with an arrest or the filing of formal charges. Ultimately, it's up to an attorney for the government to decide to charge a person with a crime. While the police can make an initial arrest, a person doesn't formally face charges until the state's attorney files them.

In second stage, an arraignment is the first court appearance. A judge or magistrate formally reads the accused person the details of the charges they're facing. They set a bond amount and conditions of bond. In rare and serious cases, they may order law enforcement to hold the person without bond until resolution of the case.

In thord stage, the defense has time and power to gather information about the case. The defense can serve a discovery demand that requires the state's attorney to produce evidence about the case. The state's attorney always has an ethical obligation to provide the defense with evidence that might be favorable to their defense.

In final stage, if the parties reach a resolution, the case may not go to trial. The state might agree to dismiss the charges, they might agree to dismiss the charges with conditions, or they might reach a plea resolution. If the parties can't resolve the case, a judge or jury may hear the evidence at a formal trial. If the jury finds the defendant not guilty, the case ends. If they find the defendant guilty, the case proceeds to sentencing.

(8) Felony and misdemeanor offenses mean

Crimes are classified as felony offenses and misdemeanor offenses. Typically, a crime is a felony if the maximum possible penalty is more than one year in jail. A felony usually brings the possibility of going to a state prison rather than a local jail. A misdemeanor is a crime that carries a maximum penalty of less than one year in jail.

Some states have low-level misdemeanors that don't carry the possibility of jail time. For example, in Michigan, a minor who drives with a blood alcohol content is guilty of a misdemeanor that's punishable by only a fine and community service. Each state may have unique classifications for a few types of offenses. For example, for certain felony offenses in Texas, offenders face only the possibility of confinement in a state jail for not less than 180 days or more than two years.

(9) What makes a law a crime?

Criminal law is the area of law that relates to prohibited conduct in society. When government leaders take steps to ban certain actions, they create crimes. Criminal law is the area of law that involves enforcing criminal law as well as defending against allegations of violations of criminal law.

The purpose of outlawing conduct is to protect society. Law makers typically pass a law with the belief that it's for the public good. Criminal laws must be applied evenly to everyone. Lawmakers can't make a law that targets only one person. The purposes of punishing criminal offenders include retribution, deterring certain behaviors, preventing additional offenses and rehabilitation of offenders.

How to cause a criminal behavior?

An act isn't a crime just because government officials prohibit the behavior. Instead, a behavior is a crime because of the penalties that are attached to a violation. In the case of a crime, a person's freedom is usually on the line. Each crime carries a maximum penalty. That penalty is the most amount of time that a person can spend in jail if they're convicted of the offense. A criminal offense often has other penalties such as a fine, probation and placing a record of the offense on a person's public, criminal history. However, the distinguishing characteristic of criminal law is that a person who commits a criminal offense might spend time in jail or prison.

(10) What are elements of a crime?

Crimes can be broken down into elements, which the prosecution must prove beyond a reasonable doubt. Criminal elements are set forth in criminal statutes, or cases in jurisdictions that allow for common-law crimes. With exceptions, every crime has at least three elements: a criminal act, also called actus reus; a criminal intent, also called mens rea; and concurrence of the two. The term conduct is often used to reflect the criminal act and intent elements.

If a crime does require a bad result, the prosecution must also prove the additional elements of causation and harm. Another requirement of some crimes is attendant circumstances. Attendant circumstances are specified factors that must be present when the crime is committed. These could include the crime's methodology, location or setting, and victim characteristics, among others.

In general case, the prosecution has to prove the elements of criminal act, criminal intent, and concurrence for attempted murder. The prosecution does not have to prove causation or that Conrad was harmed because attempt crimes, including attempted murder, do not have a bad result requirement. The criminal statute, or case in jurisdictions that allow common-law crimes, describes the criminal act element. One requirement of criminal act is that the defendant perform it voluntarily. In other words, the defendant must control the act.

Status as a Criminal Act

Generally, a defendant's status in society is not a criminal act. Status is who the defendant is, not what the defendant does. Similar to punishment for an involuntary act, when the government punishes an individual for status, it is essentially targeting that individual for circumstances that are outside his or her control. This punishment may be cruel and unusual pursuant to the Eighth Amendment if it is disproportionate to the defendant's behavior.

(11) What is criminal intent ?

Criminal intent is a necessary component of a "conventional" crime and involves a conscious decision on the part of one party to injure or deprive another. It is one of three categories of "mens rea," the basis for the establishment of guilt in a criminal case. There are multiple shades of criminal intent that may be applied in situations ranging from outright premeditation to spontaneous action.

It is possible to establish criminal intent even when a crime is not premeditated. Individuals who commit a crime spontaneously may still understand that their actions will cause harm to another party and contravene existing criminal law. In other words, an individual that takes or withholds action with the knowledge that such behavior will lead to the commission of a crime can be said to possess criminal intent.

While criminal intent is a necessary component of mens rea in virtually every modern legal system, its particulars may vary between jurisdictions. There often exists a distinction between "basic intent" and "specific intent." Since it requires a lighter burden of proof, the former is used more often to establish criminal intent.

For instance, an individual who strikes a pedestrian crossing the street in a marked crosswalk can be said to have exhibited "basic intent" whether or not they intended to cause the pedestrian harm. There are two reasons for this.

First, the driver may have ignored state and local law requiring vehicles to yield to pedestrians in crosswalks. Absent such laws, the driver either failed to pay close attention to the road ahead or assumed that the pedestrian would be able to avoid their oncoming vehicle. In either case, the driver abdicated their legal responsibility to take reasonable precautions to ensure the safety of others on the road.

"Specific intent" is invoked less frequently and often applies to cases in which the accused intends to commit a crime but has not yet done so. It may be used to justify preventive detentions associated with terrorism, treason or sabotage. For instance, an individual who has communicated his intent to assassinate an official may be judged to exhibit specific intent on the basis of his or her pronouncements.

Criminal intent may be further categorized as either "direct" or "oblique." Defined as a desire to commit a specific act in the expectation that it will result in a specific outcome, the former may be used to prove premeditation. For instance, an individual who purchases a firearm and uses it in a mugging exhibits direct intent to threaten another with deadly force.

By contrast, "oblique" intent may be used to establish guilt in cases that involve unintended consequences. An individual who undertakes a specific action with the knowledge that it may cause certain consequences can be said to have oblique intent. For instance, an individual who injures someones by firing a gun into the air near a crowd may be held responsible for that injury despite a lack of direct intent to cause harm.

Criminal intent means the intent to do something wrong or forbidden by law.

Intent refers to the state of mind accompanying an act especially a forbidden act. It is the outline of the mental pattern which is necessary to do the crime. At times criminal intent is used in the sense of mens rea-the mental element requisite for guilt of the offense charged.

Example of a case law on criminal intent. Where a person intends to kill or injure someone, but in the course of attempting to commit the crime accidentally injures or kills a third party, the defendant's criminal intent will be transferred to the third party. Under this doctrine called the Felony murder doctrine, the felonious intent involved by underlying felony may be transferred to supply intent to kill necessary to characterize the homicide as murder

(12) Why does society need criminal law?

Society needs criminal law, it may incldue these reasons: The criminal law regulates how we as individuals deal with each other and how companies and businesses, deal with us and indeed how the government local and national deals with us.The criminal law is in place to ensure that we as individuals comply with a set of rules that if we break the state will punish us.

The aim is to ensure that we do not take the law into our own hands and seek our own justice by harming the person we think has harmed us.

The purpose is for us to be protected from the actions of others by ensuring that those others are aware of an effective set of sanctions that are there to deter them from committing a crime and harming us as individuals.

It is to deter people from committing crime, however whether the punishment actually deters people from committing crime is debatable particularly in cases of sexual abuse. In those circumstances the criminal law is in place to ensure that the victims of crime are empowered to report things that have caused them harm in the past and to ensure that individuals who presents a risk to society, for example by virtue of their position of power, or other circumstances, are prevented from harming anyone in the future . If these defendants are placed in prison the reason is for public protection and often sentences are put in place to ensure this. If on the other hand people require simple punishment but not rehabilitation the deprivation of liberty, then that is the function of a prison sentence as well.

The probation service offer the possibility of rehabilitation within the community and it is often the case that such community-based options are more successful and certainly cheaper than prison based option. Public opinion in general is considered by the public as a soft option. The reality is that it is not. Defendants offending behaviour is challenged and ongoing supervision in the community is in reality a significant change to the way a person lives their life. However the perception of the public has been difficult to challenge even though the statistics show the potential for a lower reconviction rate.

The emphasis in terms of punishment has significantly changed in the past 10 years in that the victims of crime often dictate, (to an extent) the punishment and level of seriousness of the court should take into consideration. Victim impact statements are read out in court.

It is very difficult to explain to victims and family that there are punishments that are more effective than Prison. Prison sentences are getting longer and longer and the prison population is growing faster than the beds are available.

At some point the emphasis on imprisonment will have to change, simply because the financial resources are no longer available. Imprisonment, although necessary, is a very expensive way of dealing with offenders. Is it time for a rethink perhaps.? The reasons for the criminal law being so important is wide and various, the object of a good system of criminal law in my opinion is this:-

"to protect and serve the community as a whole by dealing fairly with people who cause us harm or loss, for the benefit of the community as a whole"

(13) What is Criminal Justice Reform?

Criminal justice reform is working to end the number of prisoners in the justice system through both litigation and advocacy. By fighting for nationwide reform at a variety of government levels, the nation can right wrongs before the problem becomes worse.

While no criminal justice system is entirely perfect, neither is that of the United States. Reform aims to fix these errors, and there are a number of organizations involved in the movement in various ways, including:

•Reducing harsh prison sentences
•Changing the drug sentencing policy surrounding the war on drugs
•Decriminalizing certain laws, including drug policies
•Prioritizing rehabilitation of offenders, especially juvenile offenders
•Altering policies surrounding food assistance programs and voting rights for previous offenders
•Changing minimum sentencing laws

(14) What are the three consequences , when the police arrest the defendant?

When the police arrest someone (the defendant), they take him or her to jail.

Then, 1 of 3 things happens:

• The defendant is released if the prosecutor (usually the district attorney or the city attorney) decides not to file charges; or

• The defendant posts bail (also called a "bond") or is released based on a promise to appear in court at a later date for arraignment. If either of these happen, the district attorney or police tell the defendant when to come to court for arraignment; or

• The defendant stays in jail. Law enforcement officers transport the defendant to the court

(15) How a Case Starts ?

The first step, usually, the police cite or arrest someone and write a report. This report summarizes the events leading up to the arrest or citation and provides witnesses' names and other relevant information. Defendants generally do NOT have a right to get a copy of the arrest report, but their lawyers do. The reason for this is to protect the identity of witnesses. This is another reason why it is important that a defendant charged with a misdemeanor or felony have a lawyer to represent him or her.

The second step, theprosecutor then decides whether to file charges and, if so, what charges to file. The prosecutor decides whether to charge the crime as a felony or a misdemeanor. The prosecutor can file charges on all of the crimes for which the police arrested the defendant or can decide to file fewer charges or more charges than were included in the arrest report.

The final step, because defendants have a right to a speedy trial, the prosecutor must generally file charges within 48 hours of the arrest when the defendant is in custody (in jail). Weekends, court holidays, and mandatory court closure days do not count against the 48 hours. Also, the deadline for arraignment depends on what time of the day you were arrested, so talk to a lawyer to find out exactly when the prosecutor's deadline to file charges is. All above steps are any cases are caused before all these steps are needed to passed.

(16) What does Trial mean?

Trial may need to cause that defendants in criminal cases (other than infractions) have the right to have a jury of their peers decide their guilt or innocence. Therefore, before trial, defendants need to decide whether to have a jury trial (where the jury decides if the defendant is guilty or not) or a court trial (where the judge decides). Usually, defendants choose to have a jury trial because they want a jury of their peers to hear the evidence and decide their guilt. But sometimes there may be circumstances where a defense attorney will recommend a court trial without a jury.

Everyone accused of a crime is legally presumed to be innocent until they are convicted, either by being proved guilty at a trial or by pleading guilty before trial. This means that it is the prosecutor who has to convince the jury that the defendant is guilty and must provide proof of guilt beyond a reasonable doubt. The defendant has the right to remain silent and that silence cannot be used against him or her.

(17) How to setting a Trial Date?

For a jury trial for a misdemeanor case: The law says how soon a defendant charged with a misdemeanor must be brought to trial. If the defendant is in custody at the arraignment, the trial must start within 30 days of arraignment or plea, whichever is later. If the defendant is not in custody at the arraignment, the trial must start within 45 days of arraignment or plea, whichever is later.

The defendant can "waive" (give up) the right to a speedy trial. This means the defendant agrees to have the trial after the required deadline (also known as "waiving time"). But even if the defendant waives time, the law says the trial must start within 10 days after the trial date is set. It is very important for defendants to get advice from an attorney before they waive time. The prosecutor must file the Information within 15 days of the date the defendant was "held to answer" at the preliminary hearing. The trial must start within 60 days of the arraignment on the Information. The defendant can "waive" (give up) the right to a speedy trial. This means he or she agrees to have the trial after the 60-day period (also known as "waiving time"). It is very important for defendants to get advice from an attorney before they "waive time."

(18) What Happens at Trial?

Before the trial starts, the lawyers choose a jury. The process for choosing a jury is called "voir dire." During this process the attorneys on both sides ask questions of the potential jurors to make sure the jurors will be fair and impartial.

Before the lawyers present evidence and witnesses, both sides have the right to give an opening statement about the case.

During the trial, lawyers present evidence through witnesses who testify about what they saw or know. After all the evidence is presented, the lawyers give their closing arguments.

Finally, the jury decides if the defendant is guilty or not guilty. The jury must find the defendant guilty beyond a reasonable doubt.

(19) What will occur after the trial the appeal process ?

If you are found guilty after a trial, you have the right to an appeal process. There are many reasons for an appeal of a criminal case, but appeals are also very difficult, so talk to a lawyer to make sure you know what is best for you.

There are also important deadlines that apply to appeals. If you miss the deadline, your appeal will most likely be dismissed.

For misdemeanor cases, you must file a Notice of Appeal (Misdemeanor) within 30 days of the date of the judgment or order. For felony cases, you must file a Notice of Appeal — Felony (Defendant) within 60 days of the date of the judgment or order.

Keep in mind that the appeal is not a new trial. The appellate court can review the evidence (testimony and exhibits) presented at your trial to see if the trial court made a legal error in how the testimony or exhibits were received. The appellate court does NOT decide the facts of the case as the judge or jury in the trial court does.

You can only appeal if:

1. You say there was not enough evidence in your trial to justify the verdict or judgment; and/or

2. You say there were mistakes of law during or before the trial that hurt your case.

If you say there was not enough evidence in your trial to justify the judgment, the appellate court will review the record and decide if there was substantial evidence to support the judgment. If you say mistakes of law were made, the appellate court will hold a hearing to listen to both parties. Then they will decide if there was any irregularity or mistake that prejudiced (hurt) your case. In addition to appealing after a trial, there are other situations when you can file an appeal, like appealing the validity of a plea or probation violations. Talk to your lawyer to learn more about your options to appeal.

• If you are appealing a misdemeanor conviction, you can appeal to the appellate division of the superior court. Read the Information on Appeal Procedures for Misdemeanors if you want to appeal a guilty conviction in a misdemeanor case.

• If you are appealing a felony conviction, you can appeal to the Court of Appeal in your appellate district

• If you are appealing an infraction case, read the Information on Appeal Procedures.

(20) Why do we need a criminal justice system?

The basic formation of the criminal justice system comprises of law enforcement, courts and correction. However, the pivotal role of the Criminal Justice System is to deter and investigate crime. A criminal justice system is the law and order of a society. Therefore, a strong, impartial and accountable criminal justice system, which protects the human rights of accused and victims, rich and poor, young and old alike, is the cornerstone of a just and impartial society.

The criminal justice system implemented decades ago to control the lower classes of society. Throughout the years, this system had improved to accommodate different classes, those of different status or groups of society. This implementation extends equality across all the society. The criminal justice system is a crucial part of our society and we know that comprehensive, effective, and nondiscriminatory implementation of criminal justice system powers is essential to ending violence, both for freeing individual and for ending the worldwide epidemic of violence against one another in this human race.

Why do our societies need for a criminal justice system ?

The public knows that the police cannot prevent every crime, nor apprehend every criminal. However, they expect a criminal justice system, which is reliable, effective, and respected. It must deal with cases efficiently; fight crime in each state and each town in this country. Thus, the society needs criminal justices system to protect, to deter and to prevent crime. Obviously, the idea of having a system is to ensure fairness and equality throughout a social setting.

The criminal justice system is a system that requires management by different organisations accordingly. This system consists of the police, courts and corrections. Each organisation takes responsibility of and facilitates different parts of the system to set rules or to procedures laid down by the government according to the needs of the society.

The criminal justice system is designed for a coherent administrative system for offenders. Without the threat of a punishment for wrong doing, the crime level in a society would be high. This threat that comprises of a functioning criminal justice system is a healthy threat as it brings about social order. The trauma of going through a high and complex criminal justice system turns people away from a causative culture to one of wrong doings. Punishments for crimes serve as a deterrent to criminals.

The goals of the previous criminal justice systems were mainly action based (e.g. apprehending offenders, punishing offenders and etc.). In the present era, our criminal justice system seems to be focusing on education for the public regarding crime and rehabilitation of offenders. This method is implemented to deter offenders or prevent crime from spreading. It emphasises on protecting the citizens and maintaining peace and order.

(21) Why does some one feel to need a criminal defense attorney legal service?

Why does some one want a criminal defense attorney legal service? It may include these reasons:

For property buyer case, when one property buyer needs to buy any property. The property firm company must help him to find one property lawyer to assist them to write one property contract agreement between the property firm and the property buyer in order to achieve the property purchase and sale transaction successfully.

What this means is that legal matters are litigated by putting party A against party B and letting a jury of lay people decide if the complaining party proved its case. On the criminal side, that means that the government has to prove beyond a reasonable doubt that the accused actually committed the crime. The defendant doesn't have to prove a thing...(s)he certainly doesn't have to prove innocence. The, in this tort behavioral complaining situation, the part B may choose to find one lawyer to help him to win the another A party, because the party A sues him and he fears that he will fail to win this sue in court.

Why does part A feel need to find lawyer?

Well think of the consequences of guilt. A person found guilty is branded a convict, and typically deprived of his/her liberty. Those are the direct consequences but there are collateral ones too. For example, a father put in jail won't be at home to support his family. He'll lose any job he had and it'll be all the more difficult to get one when he returns to society. People will brand him a convict and his reputation will forever be affected. Doesn't it make sense to put heavy proof requirements on the government before subjecting an accused to such punishments? So, the government ought need to help the father to find one lawyer to avoid that he needs to put in jail, because if the government feels this father will not done any criminal behavior in this case.

I think that when we give the State power to ruin someone's life and reputation, we should make them earn that power. I think we should keep the government honest. You wanna convict somebody for a crime, you gotta earn that conviction. This line of thinking seems only natural in other aspects of life, doesn't it? Consider politics. When a politician runs unopposed, doesn't it feel wrong? We want someone to oppose them. After all, a victory in a game without an opponent is hollow.

My point to all of this is that a defense attorney has not only a proper but also an important role in the American justice system. If you take away the defense attorney, you make the process of convicting someone hollow. I, for one, would like to know that when a person goes to jail it's not because of a flawed system but because he actually committed the crime.

BUT HOW CAN YOU DEFEND THE GUILTY?

Truthfully, most people acknowledge what I have stated above. They realize that a meaningful justice system allows both parties a fair fight. But it doesn't matter to them. After all, I just said it takes both sides so why not work for the prosecution? They don't understand how I could represent someone I knew to be guilty. Systemic concerns surely aren't applicable any more right? We're no longer faced with the concern of wrongful conviction, so how can I do it?

First of all, if there's going to be a determination of guilt, would you rather one defense attorney do it or twelve jurors? Maybe I learn in the course of representing my client that he's guilty. Wouldn't you rather the jury be the final voice on that, not me? I don't actually think most people want to see a system where an attorney can abandon his or her client upon learning the status of the client's guilt. And do note, I won't know up front if my client is guilty. I'd never take the police's word for it because of course they think he's guilty. No, my investigation team will do an independent investigation. As a result, it may be several months into the representation before I would know that a client is guilty. You'd really support the idea of abandoning a client halfway through the representation?

Second, representing a client constitutes so much more than just making a guilt or innocence determination. Plenty of defense attorneys negotiate plea deals for their clients each business day. That's right, a defense attorney is advising his or her client to plead guilty. We recognize that many cases will lose at trial because evidence of guilt is very strong. From this point, our job turns to ensuring that our client receives a fair sentence.

Thus, when some parties feel that they ought not have crimes, then they will seek lawyers' professional opinions to help them to win the criminal sue case more easily.

(22) What does "criminal procedure" mean ?

When a judge refers to the rules of criminal procedure, he/she is referring the rules which control how a criminal case will be handled. Rules of criminal procedure do not generally define what a violation of the law is, but rather will set out how any given criminal case will be treated as it progresses through the crminal court system. Most criminal cases will begin with an arrest. Before the police can arrest you, they must have probable cause to arrest you. Once you are arrested, you must be arraigned and informed of the charges against you. You have the right to request an attorney at arraignment. The same procedure will apply for all criminal cases.

What are Criminal Procedure Rules ?

The rules of criminal procedure are extremely important to defendants because they are designed to guarantee constitutional due process to those individuals charged with a crime. Criminal convictions can carry severe consequences, including:

?Paying steep fines and court costs

?Loss of liberty by imprisonment

?Loss of civil liberties, like the right to carry a weapon and the right to vote.

Criminal procedures are designed to make sure that any given defendant receives due process and their constitutional rights are protected. Prior to 1966, very few states had procedures in place to ensure that the constitutional rights of defendants were protected. Because of rules like these, defendants have the right to confront witnesses and the right to remain silent, even during trial.

Criminal Procedure Rule Examples

If a criminal procedure is not followed, you also have the right to challenge the admissibility of the evidence that the state would like to use against you. For example, if the police took a statement from you without providing warnings, the statement could end up being suppressed, or thrown out. Whether your case will be dismissed for a violation of criminal procedures will depend on the nature of the violation and the other evidence against you. Continuing with the same example, if your confession is the only piece of evidence against you, chances are your case will be dismissed if your confession is thrown out. However, if other evidence exists that was legally obtained, the state can proceed with the case against you—they just can't use your confession.

The rules of criminal procedure are in place to protect your rights. However, if you don't exercise them, you could lose valuable protections and remedies. Make sure to tell your attorney if you think your rights were violated and why. Failure to contest a statement taken in violation before or during your trial could result in a waiver. Waiver means that if you didn't tell the trial court your rights were violated, you are banned from bringing it up later on appeal. A lawyer in your area can review your criminal case and make sure that your rights are protected with your state's local rules of criminal procedure.

(23) How Long Does A Criminal Trial Last?

In recent years, many have the idea that criminal trials take a long time due to the high publicity of some cases that seem to have taken forever to be decided. However, most criminal trials do not take nearly as long as the popular media trials would seem to make you think. Usually the entire process from arrest to sentencing takes less than a couple of years to complete.

The first part of any trial process is the arrest phase. This begins the trial process. The arrest phase can occur at anytime within the statue of limitations for a criminal act. This means that as long as the statute of limitations is still in effect this phase of the process can occur whether it has been a few weeks or several years.

The next phase of the trial process is the arraignment phase. This portion of the process usually occurs with the defendant being brought before a judge for a formal hearing informing the defendant of the specific charges being brought against them. This part of the process usually occurs within 48 hours of a defendant's arrest in most jurisdictions. During the arraignment hearing, the judge may also decide whether to release the defendant to return for trial in the case of a misdemeanor charge or may choose to hold the defendant in the local correctional facility in the case of a felony charge. If not, there may be a detention hearing that is held later to determine if the defendant needs to be held or released.

The next phase of the trial is the preliminary hearing phase. This part of the trial process is where the prosecutor shows his or her evidence as to why the court needs to proceed with a trial. The defendant's attorney has the chance to cross-examine any witnesses and to see what exactly the evidence is that the prosecutor is going to use against his or her client. Some prosecutors however will choose to not conduct a preliminary hearing and will move straight into the Grand Jury phase of a felony trial. They may choose this to protect their witnesses and evidence so that this can be brought out in front of the Grand Jury. The preliminary hearing phase of the trial usually takes place 5-6 days after an arraignment.

The next phase of the trial is the motions and hearings phase. This usually takes about 3 months to occur but can last as long as 2 years. During this phase evidence issues are settled and investigations are conducted to determine the allowance or suppression of witnesses. Other motions may be attempted in an effort to get the case dismissed on the grounds that a speedy trial is not being conducted. Overall the motions and hearings have the possibility to delay a case for a good amount of time.

The next stage is the Grand Jury phase. In this phase a group of 16-23 citizens meet to hear the evidence presented by the prosecutor to decide if there is strong enough evidence to support an indictment. Usually the Grand Jury is a part of the prosecutor's office and as such normally hears only one side of the case. The side that they hear is the prosecutor's. The defendant has the right to testify before the Grand Jury and the defense lawyer may get permission for other witnesses to also testify. If things go in the favor of the defendant the Grand Jury may issue an indictment and the trial is over. This phase usually occurs within 6 days of the arraignment if the defendant has not waived this or if this part of the process has not been extended due to issues brought out in earlier parts of the trial. This phase is where the case is argued by the prosecutor and the defendant's attorney in front of a jury and the case is decided in favor of the prosecution or the defense. This portion of the process usually takes about a total of 4 days to 2 weeks. In extremely difficult cases it may take a few months. The Arraignment on Indictment occurs following the Grand Jury phase. This portion of the trial process is similar to the original arraignment but the charges explained will be those that the Grand Jury has issued the indictment for. This portion of the trial usually happens within about 48 hours after the indictment is issued by the Grand Jury.

The next part of the process for a felony case is to move to the motions and hearings phase where the case has evidence, witness, and Constitutional rights issues debated and settled. This part of the trial process can take anywhere from 3 months to a couple of years. Usually though the process is finished in a matter of a few months. Following this, the case moves into the trial phase. This phase of the trial process usually takes from 4 days to 2 weeks. However extremely difficult and complicated cases can take several months. This is where the jury decides the case based on the prosecutor's and defendant's attorney's arguments. Once this is done the case will move forward.

The next phase in both felony and misdemeanor cases is the Pre-Sentencing Investigation phase. This part of the trial process usually takes 1 to 12 months after the conviction to be completed. It can be delayed by up to a year should the judge decide to place the defendant on probation before sentencing. During this time, the evidence is examined and investigated to determine all of the details of the crime and its impact on the victims. Once this has been completed, the trial process moves into the sentencing phase.

The sentencing phase is the final part of the trial process. This usually occurs between 1 and 12 months after conviction. The sentencing is carried out before a judge and then the defendant is notified of the sentence that they are facing. Once this phase has finished the trial process is over unless appeals are filed for higher courts to hear the case.

In all, most cases are finished in less than a couple of years. On the federal side, the defendant is assured that their trial phase should occur within 70 days due to the Speedy Trial Act. An attorney will discuss with the defendant the timing of the case and will explain any delays that may occur. As seen throughout the explanation of this trial process though, all but the most complicated of cases are usually decided and completed in a relatively short matter of time.

CHAPTER THREE

Contract Law

(1) Contract law definition

Contact law may define as body of law that governs oral and written agreements associated with exchange of goods and services, money, and properties. It includes topics such as the nature of contractual obligations, limitation of actions, freedom of contract, privity of contract, termination of contract, and covers also agency relationships, commercial paper, and contracts of employment.

Contract may include these elements: It is an agreement with specific terms between two or more persons or entities in which there is a promise to do something in return for a valuable benefit known as consideration. Since the law of contracts is at the heart of most business dealings, it is one of the three or four most significant areas of
legal concern and can involve variations on circumstances and complexities.

The existence of a contract requires finding the following factual elements: a) an offer; b) an acceptance of that offer which results in a meeting of the minds; c) a promise to perform; d) a valuable consideration (which can be a promise or
payment in some form); e) a time or event when performance must be made (meet commitments); f) terms and conditions for performance, including fulfilling promises; g) performance.

(2) What does a unilateral contract mean?

It is one in which there is a promise to pay or give other consideration in return for actual performance.
For example, I will pay you $700 to fix my car by this week Friday; the performance is fixing the car by that date). A bilateral contract is one in which a promise is exchanged for a promise. (I promise to fix your car by

Thursday and you promise to pay $500 on Thursday).

Contracts can be either written or oral, but oral contracts are more difficult to prove and in most jurisdictions the time to sue on the contract is shorter (such as two years for oral compared to four years for written). In some cases a contract can consist of several documents, such as a series of letters, orders, offers and counteroffers.

There are a variety of types of contracts: "conditional" on an event occurring; "joint and several," in which several parties make a joint promise to perform, but each is responsible; "implied," in which the courts will determine there is a contract based on the circumstances. Parties can contract to supply all another's requirements, buy all the products made, or enter into an option to renew a contract.

The variations are almost limitless. Contracts for illegal purposes are not enforceable at law.

(3) How to cause breach of contract?

In the law of contract a breach of contract occurs when at least one party does not perform his obligations under the contract.

A statement or a clear intention that there will be no performance is often known as repudiation.

Breach results in an award of damages or specific performance.It means that failing to perform any term of a contract, written or oral, without a legitimate legal excuse. This may include not completing a job, not paying in full or on time, failure to deliver all the goods, substituting inferior or significantly different goods, not providing a bond when required, being late without excuse, or any act which shows the party will not complete the work ("anticipatory breach.") Breach of contract is one of the most common causes of law suits for damages and/or court-ordered "specific performance" of the contract

(4) Specific Performance

It means that an extraordinary equitable remedy that compels a party to execute a contract according to the precise terms agreed upon or to execute it substantially so that, under the circumstances, justice will be done between the parties.

Specific performance grants the plaintiff what he actually bargained for in the contract rather than damages (compensation for loss or injury incurred through the unlawful conduct of another) for not receiving it; thus specific performance is an equitable rather than legal remedy. By compelling the parties to perform exactly what they had agreed

to perform, more complete and perfect justice is achieved than by awarding damages for a breach of contract.

Specific performance can be granted only by a court in the exercise of its Equity powers,

subsequent to a determination of whether a valid contract that can be enforced exists and an evaluation of the relief sought.

As a general rule, specific performance is applied in breach of contract actions where monetary damages are inadequate, primarily where the contract involves land or a unique (Personal Property).Damages for the breach of a contract for the sale of ordinary personal property are, in most cases, readily recoverable so that specific performance will not be granted.

An important advantage to this remedy is that, since it is an order of an equity court,

it is supported by the enforcement power of that court. If the defendant refuses to obey that order,

the defendant will be criminal Contempt and even imprisoned. The defendant can also be cited for civil contempt for continuing to refuse to obey the order and until the defendant agrees to obey it.

(5) PRIVITY OF CONTRACT.

The relation which subsists between two contracting parties. For property buying and selling contract example, a lessee has both privity of contract and of estate; and though by an assignment of his lease he may destroy his privity

of estate, still the privity of contract remains, and he is liable on his covenant notwithstanding the assignment.

It is the relationship between the parties privy to the contract, i.e. those who are direct parties to it.

Until the passing of the Contracts (Rights of Third Parties) Act 1999, English law did not permit parties not in a relationship of privity to sue on a contract. Thus, a third party benefited by a contract could not sue on it.The effect of the Act has been to substantially relax this rule, although many contracts seeks to exclude the effect of the Act.

(6) Valid Contract

A valid contract means the remedy of specific performance presupposes the existence of a valid contract between the parties to the controversy.

The terms of the contract must be definite and certain. This is significant because equity cannot be expected
to enforce either an invalid contract in its terms that equity cannot determine exactly what it must order each party to perform.

It would be unjust for a court to compel the performance of a contract according to ambiguous terms interpreted by the court, since the court might erroneously order what the parties never intended or contemplated.

(7) Consideration means

Consideration is an essential element for the formation of a contract. It may consist of a promise to perform a desired act or a promise to refrain from doing an act that one is legally entitled to do.
In a bilateral contract—an agreement by which both parties exchange mutual promises—each promise is regarded as sufficient consideration for the other. In a unilateral contract, an agreement by which one party makes a promise in exchange for the other's performance, the performance is consideration for the promise, while the promise is consideration
for the performance.

Consideration must have a value that can be objectively determined. A promise, for example, to make a gift or a promise of love or affection is not enforceable because of the subjective nature of the promise.Thus, consideration needs have these elements , they include: 1) payment or money. 2) a vital element in the law of contracts,
consideration is a benefit which must be bargained for between the parties, and is the essential reason for a party entering into a contract. Consideration must be of value (at least to the parties), and is exchanged for the performance or promise
of performance by the other party (such performance itself is consideration).

In a contract, one consideration (thing given) is exchanged for another consideration.
Not doing an act (forbearance) can be consideration, such as "I will pay you $1,000 not to build a road next to my fence," So, consideration needs have that which is used to hide the true amount being paid.
Contracts may become unenforceable or rescindable (undone by rescission) for "failure of consideration" when the intended consideration is found to worth less than expected, is damaged or destroyed, or performance is not made properly

(as when the mechanic does not make the car run properly). Acts which are illegal or so immoral that they are against established public policy cannot serve as consideration for enforceable contracts. Examples: prostitution, gambling where outlawed, or

inducing someone to breach an agreemen or a promise.

(8) What are the essential characterists of a contract agreement?

To constitute a legal contract, an agreement must have all of the following 5 characteristics:

They may include as below:

A contract must have a legal purpose to be enforceable. For example, Johnny hires Paul to kill Peter. Johny drafts an agreement outlining Paul's responsibilities, namely to acquire a gun and shoot Peter in the head. The agreement also specifies the amount Johnny will pay Paul once Peter

is dead. A contract of murder for hire is illegal. If Paul fails to fulfill his obligations under the agreement,

Johnny will have no consideration or payment responsibity against Paul. The agreement Johnny has drafted is unenforceable.

A contract must have Mutual Agreement. All parties to the contract must have reached a "meeting of the minds." That is, one party must have extended an offer to which the other parties have agreed. For example, Johnny signs a contract with Peter Tree Trimming. The contract outlines the scope of the work Peter will perform on Johnny's property.

Johnny and Peter have a mutual agreement regarding the work that will be done.

A contract must have Consideration. Each party to the contract must agree to give up something of value in exchange for a benefit.For example, you hire an independent contractor to repave your driveway. You and the independent contractor sign an agreement in which you promise to pay a sum of money in exchange for the paving work. Both you and the contractor have agreed to give up something

of value. You have agreed to pay money, and the contractor has agreed to perform the paving work.

A contact must have Competent Parties. The parties to a contract must be competent. That is, they must be of sound mind,of legal age, and without sign by drugs or alcohol influence. If you enter into a contract with a minor or an insane person, the contract will not be enforced.

A contract must have Genuine Assent. All parties must engage in the agreement freely. A contract may not be enforced if mistakes have been made by one or more parties. Likewise, a contract may be voided if one party has committed fraud or exerted undue influence over another. For example, you sign a contract in which you agree to sell your house to your next-door neighbor for one million. When you signed the contract, your neighbor was pointing a gun at your head. Clearly, you made the agreement under duress, so the contract is not valid, because you sign your house selling agreement from your nexr door neighbor's force behavior.

(9) When does one contract effective date?

The Effective Date or Effectiveness of Agreement clause sets the date when the rights and obligations under the agreement become operational. The Effective Date need not be the same as the execution date. In the absence of an effective date, the terms of the agreement become operational upon execution.Are Contracts That Don't Specify a Date Still Legal?

There are some potential points when you enter into a contract with a vendor or client, especially if you have a contract with no end date_._ While the contract is likely valid, it must detail enough information to outline the agreement
and must include the signatures of all parties involved. A contract does not need a date to be valid. Most times, it will simply begin on the day it is signed.

Consideration on one contract effective date, it includes these points as below:

Contract Start Date Considerations, in the absence of a contract expiration date,
it's sometimes confusing to know when a contract begins. In most instances, written contracts that don't
specify an effective date begin on the contract signing date. Oral contracts, however, are effective the day that one party accepted the other party's offer because no contract signing date exists.
In cases in which the parties involved can't remember the contract signing date then a court will have to determine the effective date by examining other documents related to the agreement, and the actions of each party.

Contract End Date Considerations, when a written agreement lacks a contract expiration date,
and a dispute arises about when the contract ends, a court must examine all aspects of the agreement
to determine when the agreement ended or will end. If you signed a contract to buy laptops from a vendor,
for example, a court may determine that the contract expiration date occurred when the supplier delivered the laptops to your business. The court could confirm this by reviewing the receipt of delivery to determine
that the contract was completed. In most instances, courts will apply the standard of a "reasonable period
of time" based on the terms of the agreement to determine the logical ending of a contract.

Time-Sensitive Contracts, it means that in some instances, two parties may enter into a contract that
requires payment on every anniversary of the contract start date. A dispute may arise, however,
if there is no written start date. In that instance, a court may default to the day that the parties signed the contract, or in the event of an oral contract, the date an offer was accepted. If neither party is able to remember the date the contract was signed, the court may have to determine the date the first payment was made, and use that date as the anniversary date for each subsequent year.

CHAPTER FOUR

USA contract law and UK contract and tort law principle

Overview of USA Contract Law and UK Contract and Tort Law Principles

In English contract law, a contract is defined as a legally binding agreement between two or more parties that creates obligations enforceable by law.

For a contract to be legally binding, it must contain four essential elements: Offer, Acceptance, Consideration, and Intention to create legal relations.

1. The Four Essential Elements

A. Offer

An expression of willingness to contract on specific terms, made with the intention that it shall become binding as soon as it is accepted by the person to whom it is addressed.

Case Study: Carlill v Carbolic Smoke Ball Co [1893]

Facts: The company advertised that they would pay £100 to anyone who caught influenza after using their smoke ball as directed. Mrs. Carlill used it, caught the flu, and sued.

Principle: The court held that an advertisement can be a unilateral offer to the world. By performing the conditions (using the smoke ball), Mrs. Carlill accepted the offer.

B. Acceptance

A final and unqualified expression of assent to the terms of an offer. It must be communicated to the offeror.

Case Study: Hyde v Wrench [1840]

Facts: Wrench offered to sell a farm for £1,000. Hyde offered £950. Wrench refused. Hyde then tried to accept the original £1,000 offer.

Principle: A counter-offer kills the original offer. Once Hyde made a counter-offer of £950, the original offer of £1,000 ceased to exist and could no longer be accepted.

C. Consideration

Something of value must be exchanged between the parties. It does not need to be adequate (fair market value), but it must be "sufficient" (have some legal value).

Case Study: Chappell & Co Ltd v Nestlé Co Ltd [1960]

Facts: Nestlé offered a record in exchange for money and three chocolate bar wrappers.

Principle: The court held that the wrappers were part of the consideration, even though they had little intrinsic value. Consideration must be sufficient, but it need not be adequate.

D. Intention to Create Legal Relations

The parties must intend for the agreement to be legally enforceable. In commercial agreements, there is a presumption that it is binding. In social or domestic agreements, there is a presumption that it is not binding.

Case Study: Balfour v Balfour [1919]

Facts: A husband promised to pay his wife £30 a month while he was working abroad. When he stopped paying, she sued.

Principle: The court held that domestic agreements between spouses are generally not intended to be legally binding.

2. Other Important Concepts

Capacity

Parties must have the legal ability to enter a contract (e.g., they must be over 18 and of sound mind).

Privity of Contract

Generally, only the parties to a contract can sue or be sued under it.

Exception: The Contracts (Rights of Third Parties) Act 1999 allows a third party to enforce a contract if the contract expressly provides for it or confers a benefit on them.

Vitiating Factors (Why a contract might be void)

Even if the four elements exist, a contract can be set aside due to:

Misrepresentation: A false statement of fact that induces a party to enter a contract.

Duress/Undue Influence: Being forced or pressured into a contract.

Mistake: A fundamental error regarding thc subject matter.

3. Breach of Contract

When one party fails to perform their obligations, the other party may seek remedies:

Damages: Monetary compensation (the most common remedy). The goal is to put the claimant in the position they would have been in had the contract been performed (Robinson v Harman [1848]).

Specific Performance: A court order requiring the party to actually perform their contractual duty (rare, usually only for unique items like land or art).

Rescission: Canceling the contract and returning parties to their pre-contractual state.

Disclaimer: This summary is for educational purposes and does not constitute legal advice. Contract law is complex and fact-specific; for legal issues, consult a qualified solicitor.

Key Principles of USA Contract Law

1. Uniform Commercial Code (UCC)

In the United States, the **Uniform Commercial Code (UCC)**governs commercial transactions, particularly those involving the sale of goods. The UCC establishes a framework that promotes consistency across states, ensuring that contracts are interpreted uniformly. It imposes an obligation of good faith in performance and enforcement under UCC 1-304, which is often implied into contracts even if not explicitly stated.

2. Good Faith Obligations

The duty of good faith in the U.S. legal system is more structured compared to English law. Every commercial contract governed by the UCC includes this duty, which requires parties to act honestly and fairly towards each other.

3. Limitation of Liability

U.S. courts generally enforce limitation of liability clauses as long as they are clear and unambiguous. Indemnity provisions often include duties to defend and hold harmless[1]. Additionally, indirect and consequential losses are commonly interpreted to include lost profits due to a breach.

4. Material Breach

In U.S. law, a **material breach**occurs when a breach substantially defeats the purpose of the contract or deprives a party of expected benefits. This definition is more rigid than in English law, where courts conduct a fact-specific analysis.

5. Punitive Damages

Punitive damages are awarded more frequently in the United States than in England, primarily as a means to punish wrongful conduct beyond mere compensation for losses. However, punitive damages for breach of contract are typically only available if accompanied by an independent tort.

Key Principles of UK Contract Law

1. Good Faith

Unlike U.S. law, English law does not recognize an overarching duty of good faith in contracts except in certain relational contracts where long-term relationships exist. Courts may imply such duties based on specific circumstances but do not impose them universally.

2. Reasonable vs Best Endeavours

English law distinguishes between "reasonable endeavours" and "best endeavours." The former requires taking reasonable steps without sacrificing one's own interests, while the latter demands all possible efforts even at significant inconvenience or cost. In contrast, U.S. courts often use "best efforts" without making this distinction.

3. Limitation of Liability

In England, limitation clauses must be reasonable under The Unfair Contract Terms Act 1977 (UCTA) when dealing with consumers or other businesses. Clear language is required for these clauses to be enforceable.

4. Material Breach

English law takes a flexible approach to defining material breaches; it does not require that a breach go to the root of the contract but considers various factors including impact on the innocent party.

5. Punitive Damages

Punitive damages are rarely awarded under English law except in tort cases involving willful misconduct or dishonesty. They are not available for breaches of contract regardless of severity.

Key Principles of Tort Law

USA Tort Law

Tort law in the United States allows for claims based on negligence or intentional wrongdoing that causes harm to another party. The system emphasizes compensatory damages aimed at making victims whole rather than punitive measures unless tied to independent torts like fraud.

UK Tort Law

UK tort law similarly focuses on compensatory damages but has stricter rules regarding liability and causation compared to U.S. standards[1]. For example, claims for defamation have different thresholds for public figures versus private individuals.

Conclusion

While both U.S. and UK laws share foundational principles rooted in common law traditions, significant differences exist regarding good faith obligations, limitation clauses, definitions of material breach, punitive damages availability, and tort liability standards.

Understanding these differences is essential for effective legal compliance and risk management when engaging in cross-border transactions between these two jurisdictions.

The differences between USA and UK contract law are significant, reflecting the distinct legal frameworks and interpretations that have evolved in each jurisdiction. Below are some of the key areas where these differences manifest.

1. Good Faith Obligations

In the United States, there is a general duty of good faith in the performance and enforcement of contracts, particularly under the Uniform Commercial Code (UCC) 1-304. This duty is often implied into commercial contracts, especially those involving the sale of goods. In contrast,**English law does not recognize a general duty of good faith across all contracts**, although it may be implied in specific types of relational contracts that require long-term relationships and mutual trust.

2. Reasonable vs. Best Endeavours

English law distinguishes between "reasonable endeavours" and "best endeavours."The former requires parties to take reasonable steps without sacrificing their own commercial interests, while the latter demands that parties take all steps within their power to achieve a goal, even at considerable inconvenience or expense.**In the US, however, courts typically use "best efforts" without making a distinction between these two standards**, interpreting it based on contract language and industry norms.

3. Limitation of Liability

Both jurisdictions enforce limitation of liability clauses but with different nuances. In England, such clauses must be reasonable under the Unfair Contract Terms Act 1977 when dealing with consumers; however, this act does not apply to international supply contracts unless specified otherwise. 聽**In the US, courts also uphold clear and unambiguous limitation clauses but often include indemnity provisions that may encompass duties to defend against claims**, which is less common in English law.

4. Material Breach

The concept of material breach differs significantly between the two systems. In England, there is no strict definition; courts assess breaches based on various factors related to the contract's nature and impact on the innocent party. Conversely,**the US applies a more rigid definition**, where a material breach occurs when it substantially defeats the purpose of the contract or deprives a party of expected benefits.

5. Assignment and Novation

While both legal systems recognize assignment and novation, they interpret them differently. In England, an assignment transfers rights but not obligations unless explicitly stated; in contrast,**in the US, an assignment can transfer both rights and obligations**, although the original party remains liable unless there is a novation that releases them from liability.

6. Punitive Damages

Punitive damages are awarded more frequently in the United States than in England. In English law, punitive damages are rare and generally only applicable in tort cases involving willful misconduct; they are not available for breach of contract cases at all.**In contrast, US courts may award punitive damages for breaches if they involve independent torts like fraud**, with juries determining these awards.

Conclusion

Understanding these key differences is crucial for businesses operating across borders as they navigate contractual agreements effectively within each jurisdiction's legal framework.

Differences in Contract Formation Between the USA and UK

Contract formation in the USA and UK differs primarily in terms of legal principles, requirements for consideration, and the implications of good faith.

1. Legal Framework

Both the USA and UK derive their contract law from common law traditions; however, they have developed distinct legal frameworks. In the USA, the Uniform Commercial Code (UCC) governs commercial contracts across states, providing a standardized set of rules that facilitate interstate commerce. The UCC emphasizes flexibility and allows for contracts to be formed even when some terms are left open or ambiguous, as long as there is a clear intent to create a contract.

In contrast, UK contract law does not have an equivalent to the UCC. Instead, it relies on a combination of statutes and case law. This means that while UK contracts can also be flexible, they often require more precision in terms of language and clarity regarding obligations.

2. Consideration

Consideration is a fundamental element required for contract formation in both jurisdictions; however, its application varies slightly. In both the USA and UK, consideration must be present for a contract to be enforceable. This means that each party must provide something of value—be it money, services, or goods—in exchange for what they receive.

However, US courts may sometimes recognize "promissory estoppel," which allows enforcement of a promise even without consideration if one party reasonably relied on that promise to their detriment. The UK does not generally recognize promissory estoppel in the same way; instead, it adheres strictly to the requirement of consideration.

3. Good Faith Obligations

Another significant difference lies in the obligation of good faith during contract performance. Under US law, particularly as outlined by the UCC

(Section 1-304), there is an implied duty of good faith that applies to all commercial contracts. This means parties are expected to act honestly and fairly towards each other throughout the duration of their agreement.

Conversely, English law does not impose a general duty of good faith across all contracts. While certain types of contracts may imply such duties (like relational contracts), this is not universally applicable. As such, parties in England may have less protection against opportunistic behavior compared to their counterparts in the USA.

4. Acceptance and Offer

The process of offer and acceptance also shows differences between these two legal systems. In both jurisdictions, an offer must be clear enough that acceptance creates a binding agreement. However, US courts tend to adopt a more liberal approach regarding what constitutes an acceptable offer or acceptance compared to UK courts. For instance, US courts may allow for acceptance through conduct rather than explicit verbal or written agreement.

In contrast, UK law requires more formalities in certain situations (e.g., land transactions) where specific forms must be adhered to for a valid contract.

Conclusion

In summary, **contract formation differs between the USA and UK primarily due to variations in legal frameworks governing contracts (UCC vs common law), treatment of consideration (including promissory estoppel), obligations regarding good faith during performance, and approaches to offer and acceptance.** Understanding these differences is crucial for businesses operating across these jurisdictions.

Key Elements of Contract Formation in the USA Compared to the UK

Contract formation is a fundamental aspect of both US and UK law, and while there are many similarities due to their common law roots, there are also significant differences. Understanding these elements is crucial for businesses and individuals engaging in contractual agreements across these jurisdictions.

1. Offer and Acceptance

In both the USA and the UK, a contract begins with an offer made by one party (the offeror) that is accepted by another party (the offeree). The offer must be clear enough that the offeree understands what is being proposed.

- **USA:** The acceptance must mirror the terms of the offer exactly; any deviation constitutes a counter-offer rather than acceptance. This principle is often referred to as the "mirror image rule."
- **UK:** Similar principles apply, but there is more flexibility regarding acceptance. For example, acceptance can occur through conduct rather than just explicit agreement.

2. Consideration

Consideration refers to something of value that is exchanged between parties, which is necessary for a contract to be enforceable.

- **USA:** Consideration must be present for a contract to be valid; it can take various forms such as money, services, or promises. The concept of "mutuality of obligation" means both parties must provide consideration.
- **UK:** The requirement for consideration is also present; however, certain types of contracts (like deeds) may not require consideration to be enforceable.

3. Intention to Create Legal Relations

Both legal systems require that parties intend their agreement to have legal consequences.

- **USA:** There is generally a presumption that commercial agreements are intended to create legal relations unless explicitly stated otherwise.

- **UK**: In contrast, social or domestic agreements are presumed not to create legal relations unless proven otherwise. This distinction can affect enforcement significantly.

4. Capacity

The parties involved must have the legal capacity to enter into a contract.

- **USA**: Individuals must be of sound mind and at least 18 years old (with some exceptions). Contracts entered into by minors may be voidable.
- **UK**: Similar rules apply regarding age and mental capacity; however, contracts with minors may still be binding if they are for necessities.

5. Legality

The purpose of the contract must be lawful for it to be enforceable in both jurisdictions.

- **USA**: Contracts formed for illegal purposes are void ab initio (invalid from the outset).
- **UK**: Likewise, any agreement that involves illegal activities cannot be enforced by law.

Conclusion

In summary, while both US and UK contract law share foundational principles regarding offer and acceptance, consideration, intention to create legal relations, capacity, and legality, they differ in nuances such as how acceptance can occur and assumptions about intent in different contexts. Understanding these distinctions is essential for effective contract management across borders.

The key elements of contract formation in the USA compared to the UK include:

1. Offer and Acceptance

2. Consideration
3. Intention to Create Legal Relations
4. Capacity
5. Legality

Key Differences Between UK and US Business Law

Both the United Kingdom (UK) and the United States (US) operate under common law systems, but there are significant differences in their business laws that affect how companies operate, contract, and resolve disputes. Understanding these differences is crucial for businesses engaging in cross-border transactions or operations.

1. Contract Law

One of the most notable differences lies in contract law. In the US, there is a general duty of good faith implied in all commercial contracts as per the Uniform Commercial Code (UCC) § 1-304. This means that parties are expected to perform their contractual obligations honestly and fairly. Conversely, English law does not recognize a general duty of good faith; it may only be implied in specific types of contracts known as relational contracts[1].

2. Employment Law

Employment laws differ significantly between the two jurisdictions. The US predominantly follows an "at-will" employment doctrine, allowing employers to terminate employees without cause or notice, unless otherwise specified in a contract. In contrast, UK employment law requires justifiable reasons for termination and provides employees with rights against unfair dismissal after two years of service[2].

3. Liability Limitations

In terms of liability limitations, both jurisdictions enforce exclusion clauses in contracts; however, English law requires that such clauses be clear and unambiguous to be enforceable under the Unfair Contract Terms Act 1977 (UCTA). The UCTA also restricts liability exclusions when dealing with consumers[3]. In the US, courts generally uphold limitation clauses as long as they do not violate public policy.

4. Assignment and Novation

The treatment of assignment differs between the two legal systems. In England, an assignment transfers only rights under a contract without transferring obligations unless explicitly stated[4]. In contrast, US law allows for both rights and obligations to be assigned unless prohibited by the contract itself[5]. Both jurisdictions agree on novation requiring consent from all parties involved.

5. Punitive Damages

Punitive damages are awarded more frequently in the US than in England. In the US legal system, punitive damages can be awarded not only for tortious conduct but also in some breach of contract cases if accompanied by an independent tort like fraud[6]. However, English law rarely awards punitive damages for breaches of contract; they are primarily reserved for tort cases involving willful misconduct[7].

6. Corporate Structure and Regulation

Corporate formation also varies significantly between the two countries. The UK has a centralized registration system through Companies House where all companies must register[8]. In contrast, corporations in the US are formed at the state level with no central registry; each state has its own regulations governing corporate formation and operation[9].

Conclusion

Understanding these key differences is essential for businesses operating across borders to ensure compliance with local laws and mitigate risks associated with international operations.

Differences in Contract Law Between the UK and the US

Contract law in the United Kingdom and the United States, while both rooted in common law traditions, exhibits significant differences in various aspects. Understanding these differences is crucial for businesses operating across these jurisdictions.

1. Good Faith Obligations

In the United States, there is a general duty of good faith and fair dealing that applies to all contracts under the Uniform Commercial Code (UCC) § 1-304. This duty is often implied into commercial contracts, particularly those involving the sale of goods. Conversely, English law does not recognize a broad duty of good faith. It may imply such a duty only in specific types of contracts known as "relational contracts," which require long-term relationships and mutual trust.

2. Endeavours Clauses

The terminology surrounding efforts to fulfill contractual obligations differs significantly between the two legal systems. In England, "reasonable endeavours" and "best endeavours" are distinct legal standards. "Reasonable endeavours" requires taking reasonable steps without sacrificing one's own commercial interests, while "best endeavours" demands all possible efforts even at considerable inconvenience. In contrast, U.S. law typically employs the term "best efforts," which lacks a formal distinction between reasonable and best efforts; its interpretation depends on contract language and industry standards.

3. Limitation of Liability

Both jurisdictions enforce limitation of liability clauses but with different nuances. In England, such clauses must be clear and reasonable under the Unfair Contract Terms Act 1977 (UCTA), especially when dealing with consumers. UCTA does not apply to international supply contracts unless specifically stated. In the U.S., courts also enforce limitation clauses if they are unambiguous and not against public policy; however, indemnity provisions often include broader protections like duties to defend.

4. Material Breach

The concept of material breach varies between the two systems. English law does not have a strict definition for material breach; instead, it relies on a fact-specific analysis considering various factors related to the contract's nature and obligations. The U.S., however, has a more rigid definition where a material breach substantially defeats the contract's purpose or deprives one party of expected benefits.

5. Assignment and Novation

While both legal systems recognize novation as transferring both rights and obligations with consent from all parties involved, their treatment of assignment differs slightly. In England, an assignment transfers rights without automatically transferring obligations unless explicitly stated. In contrast, U.S. law allows assignments to transfer both rights and obligations but keeps original parties secondarily liable unless otherwise specified.

6. Punitive Damages

Punitive damages are awarded much more frequently in U.S. courts compared to English courts where they are rare and generally limited to tort cases involving willful misconduct. In breach of contract cases in England, punitive damages are not available at all; whereas in the U.S., they can be awarded if tied to an independent tort like fraud.

Conclusion

In summary, while both UK and US contract laws share foundational similarities due to their common law roots, they diverge significantly in areas such as good faith obligations, definitions of effort standards, limitation of liability interpretations, concepts of material breach, assignment practices, and approaches to punitive damages. Businesses engaging internationally must navigate these differences carefully to ensure compliance and protection under applicable laws.

Similarities Between UK and US Contract Laws

While there are significant differences between contract laws in the UK and the US, there are also several key similarities.

Enforcement of Exclusion and Limitation of Liability Clauses

Both UK and US laws enforce exclusion and limitation of liability clauses in contracts between commercial parties, provided that such clauses are clear, unambiguous, and not against public policy.In England, courts have enforced exclusions and limitations of liability clauses and indemnities in contracts between commercial parties governed by English law, subject to some exceptions on public policy grounds. Similarly, in the US, courts are inclined to enforce exclusion and limitation of liability and indemnity clauses, particularly when these clauses are clear, unambiguous, and not contrary to public policy.

Obligation to Use Good Faith

Both UK and US laws recognize the concept of good faith in contract performance and enforcement. While the US has a more structured approach to the duty of good faith, with every commercial contract implying a duty of good faith in performance and enforcement under the Uniform Commercial Code (UCC) §1-304,English law does not recognize an overarching duty of good faith in contracts but may imply a duty of good faith in "relational contracts."

Novation

Both UK and US laws share the same interpretation of a "novation." A novation fully releases the original contracting party from liability and requires the consent of all parties to the contract.This means that if a party wants to transfer both the rights and obligations in a contract while also releasing the original party from any obligation to perform, a novation is required.

Punitive Damages

Both UK and US laws have similar approaches to punitive damages in certain situations. In England, punitive damages are rare and typically only awarded in limited circumstances, such as in tort cases where the defendant has acted willfully or dishonestly. In the US, punitive damages are awarded more frequently, but typically not for breach of contract unless the breach constitutes an independent tort.

Interpretation of Contracts

Both UK and US laws have similar approaches to contract interpretation. In both jurisdictions, contracts are interpreted based on their plain meaning, and the intentions of the parties are considered. However, there are differences in the approach to interpreting ambiguous clauses, with English law taking a more literal approach and US law considering the context and circumstances surrounding the contract.

The key similarities between contract laws in the UK and the US include the enforcement of exclusion and limitation of liability clauses, the recognition of good faith in contract performance and enforcement, the interpretation of novation, and approaches to punitive damages and contract interpretation.

Differences in Breach of Contract Remedies in the UK and US

The remedies available for breach of contract in the United Kingdom and the United States exhibit several key differences, shaped by their respective legal traditions and practices. Understanding these differences is crucial for parties engaged in contracts across these jurisdictions.

Types of Damages

Compensatory Damages: Both jurisdictions primarily aim to provide compensatory damages to the injured party, which are designed to put them in the position they would have been in had the contract been performed. However, there are nuances:

In the UK, damages are generally classified as either general or special damages. General damages cover losses that naturally arise from a breach, while special damages must be specifically pleaded and proven.

In the US, compensatory damages can include both direct and consequential damages. Consequential damages refer to losses that occur as a foreseeable result of the breach but are not directly caused by it. The distinction between direct and consequential losses is more pronounced in US law.

Punitive Damages

Punitive Damages:

In the US, punitive damages may be awarded in cases where a party's conduct is found to be particularly egregious or malicious. These are intended to punish the wrongdoer and deter similar behavior in the future.

Conversely, punitive damages are very rare in the UK. They are typically only awarded in tort cases involving willful misconduct or fraud, not for breaches of contract.

Mitigation of Damages

Duty to Mitigate:

Both jurisdictions impose a duty on the non-breaching party to mitigate their losses; however, how this duty is interpreted can differ.

In the UK, if a claimant fails to take reasonable steps to mitigate their loss, they may find their recovery reduced accordingly.

In the US, while there is also a duty to mitigate, courts may allow for broader interpretations regarding what constitutes reasonable mitigation efforts.

Specific Performance

Specific Performance:

In both jurisdictions, specific performance (an order requiring a party to fulfill their contractual obligations) can be granted but under different circumstances.

The UK courts tend to grant specific performance more readily than US courts, especially when monetary damages would not suffice (e.g., unique goods or property).

In contrast, US courts often view specific performance as an extraordinary remedy and may require clear evidence that monetary compensation would be inadequate.

Limitation Periods

Limitation Periods for Claims:

The limitation periods within which claims must be brought differ significantly between jurisdictions.

In the UK, most contract claims must be brought within six years from when the cause of action arose.

In many US states, limitation periods vary widely; for example, some states allow only four years for breach of contract claims.

Conclusion

In summary, while both UK and US legal systems aim to provide remedies for breach of contract primarily through compensatory damages, significant differences exist regarding punitive damages, mitigation duties, specific performance availability, and limitation periods. Understanding these distinctions is essential for effective contract management across these jurisdictions.

The main differences in breach of contract remedies between the UK and US include variations in types of damages (including punitive damage availability), approaches to mitigation duties, specific performance enforcement practices, and differing limitation periods for filing claims.

Although contract law in both jurisdictions originates from common law traditions, key differences have developed over time.

M&A practices highlight further divergences between UK and US approaches regarding representations and warranties during transactions.

Introduction to Breach of Contract Remedies

In the event of a breach of contract, the affected party may seek various remedies to mitigate their losses. The UK and US legal systems provide several options for breach of contract remedies, which have been shaped by significant legal precedents.

UK Legal Precedents

The UK courts have established several key precedents regarding breach of contract remedies. One notable case is Hedley Byrne & Co Ltd v Heller & Partners Ltd (1964), which established the principle of "duty of care" in contract law.[1] This case held that a party owes a duty of care to the other party in contractual negotiations, and a breach of this duty can lead to damages.

Another significant case is Lombard North Central plc v Butterworth (1987), which clarified the concept of "repudiation" in contract law.The court held that a repudiatory breach can terminate the contract, and the innocent party can claim damages.

US Legal Precedents

In the US, the courts have also established important precedents regarding breach of contract remedies. One landmark case is Hadley v Baxendale (1850), which set the standard for damages in breach of contract cases.[3] The court held that damages should be awarded based on the "natural and probable consequences" of the breach.

Another notable case is Poussard v. Spiers and Pond (1876), which established the concept of "anticipatory breach" in contract law. The court held that a party can treat a contract as breached if the other party indicates that they will not perform their obligations.

Remedies for Breach of Contract

Both UK and US courts offer various remedies for breach of contract, including:

Damages: monetary compensation for losses suffered due to the breach

Specific Performance: a court order requiring the breaching party to perform their obligations

Injunctions: a court order restraining the breaching party from continuing the breach

Rescission: cancellation of the contract

Conclusion

In conclusion, the UK and US legal systems have established significant precedents regarding breach of contract remedies. These precedents provide guidance on the available remedies and the principles for awarding damages.

The remedies for breach of contract in the UK and US include damages, specific performance, injunctions, and rescission, and the courts consider factors such as the severity of the breach, the parties' intentions, and the consequences of the breach when determining the appropriate remedy.

Influence of Recent Court Cases on Breach of Contract Laws in the UK and US

Recent court cases in both the UK and the US have significantly influenced breach of contract laws, particularly regarding the interpretation of contractual terms, the enforcement of force majeure clauses, and the implications of implied terms. These developments highlight a trend towards greater clarity and specificity in contract drafting, as well as a judicial willingness to uphold parties' intentions as expressed in their agreements.

UK Developments

In the UK, notable cases such as RTI Ltd v MUR Shipping BV have clarified how force majeure clauses are interpreted. The Supreme Court ruled that a party invoking a force majeure clause does not have to accept non-contractual performance unless explicitly required by the contract. This decision emphasized that parties must draft their contracts with precision to avoid ambiguity regarding obligations during unforeseen events. The court underscored that reasonable endeavours provisions do not compel acceptance of alternative performance if it deviates from what was originally agreed upon.

Another significant case is Tesco Stores Ltd v USDAW, where the Supreme Court ruled against Tesco's attempt to terminate employees' rights to retained pay through a "fire and rehire" strategy. The court found that such actions breached an implied term in employment contracts, reinforcing that employers cannot unilaterally alter fundamental contractual benefits without mutual consent. This case illustrates how courts are increasingly protecting employee rights within contractual frameworks.

US Developments

In the US, recent rulings have similarly focused on enforcing clear contractual terms. For instance, courts have upheld exclusion clauses when they are clearly articulated, emphasizing that parties should be cautious about relying on implied terms or construction arguments to escape liability. This aligns with trends seen in UK law where clarity in contract language is paramount.

Moreover, cases involving force majeure claims due to events like COVID-19 have shown that courts require substantial evidence linking the event directly to an inability to perform contractual obligations. In PD Teesport Ltd v P&O North Sea Ferries Ltd, for example, the High Court rejected a force majeure argument based on Brexit because there was insufficient evidence demonstrating its impact on performance. This reflects a rigorous standard for proving force majeure claims in both jurisdictions.

Conclusion

Overall, recent court decisions in both the UK and US emphasize the importance of precise language in contracts and reinforce judicial reluctance to intervene where parties have clearly defined their rights and obligations. As businesses navigate these legal landscapes, they must ensure their contracts are comprehensive and unambiguous to mitigate risks associated with breaches.

In summary, recent court cases have reinforced the necessity for clarity and specificity in contract drafting while also highlighting judicial support for upholding explicit contractual agreements over implied terms or opportunistic interpretations.

Landmark Court Cases Shaping Breach of Contract Laws

Breach of contract laws in both the UK and the US have been significantly influenced by landmark court cases that established key principles and precedents. Below are some notable cases from each jurisdiction.

United Kingdom

1. Offer and Acceptance

Case: Carlill v Carbolic Smoke Ball Co [1893] 1 QB 256

The Facts: The company advertised a "smoke ball" claiming it would prevent influenza and offered a £100 reward to anyone who used it and still caught the flu. Mrs. Carlill used it, caught the flu, and sued for the money.

The company argued the ad was "mere puffery" and not a binding contract.

The Principle: The court held that an advertisement can constitute a unilateral offer to the world. By performing the conditions (using the product), the offeree accepts the offer. It established that you do not need to notify the offeror of your acceptance in a unilateral contract.

This case is foundational in establishing the principles of offer, acceptance, and consideration in contract law. The court ruled that an advertisement constituted a unilateral offer to the public, which could be accepted by anyone who performed the conditions stated in the ad (using the smoke ball as directed). This case clarified how offers can be made and accepted, impacting breach of contract interpretations when obligations are not met.

Breach of Contract: Williams v. Roffey Bros & Nicholls (Contractors) Ltd (1990)

In this case, it was determined that a promise to pay more for work already contracted could be enforceable if it confers a practical benefit to the promisor. The ruling emphasized that consideration does not always need to be new or additional; rather, it can arise from fulfilling existing contractual duties under certain circumstances.

Stilk v. Myrick (1809)

This case established that a promise made without new consideration is generally unenforceable. The court ruled that sailors who were promised extra pay for completing their voyage after some crew members deserted had no legal grounds for claiming additional wages since they were already obligated to complete their duties.

Drax Power Ltd v Wipro Ltd (2023)

A recent case where the interpretation of liability caps in contracts was scrutinized. The court found that a clause limiting liability applied to all claims collectively rather than per event, emphasizing the importance of precise drafting in contracts.

United States

Hadley v. Baxendale (1854)

This seminal case established the rule for consequential damages in breach of contract cases. The court held that damages must arise naturally from the breach or be within the contemplation of both parties at the time they made the contract. This principle has guided courts in determining recoverable damages ever since.

Lucy v. Zehmer (1954)

In this case, an informal agreement made during a social gathering was deemed enforceable because one party believed it to be serious and binding at the time of agreement. The ruling highlighted how intent and understanding between parties can affect contract validity and breach implications.

Restatement (Second) of Contracts

Although not a single case, this influential document summarizes American contract law principles including those related to breach of contract, offering guidance on issues such as performance standards and remedies available upon breach. Courts often refer to this Restatement when adjudicating disputes.

Katz v. Oak Industries Inc (1988)

This case involved issues surrounding implied contracts and good faith dealings within commercial transactions, reinforcing expectations around performance standards and obligations under contracts.

Consideration (The "Price" of the Promise)

Case: Currie v Misa (1875) LR 10 Ex 153

The Principle: This case provided the classic definition of consideration: "A valuable consideration, in the sense of the law, may consist either in some right, interest, profit, or benefit accruing to the one party, or some forbearance, detriment, loss, or responsibility, given, suffered, or undertaken by the other." Essentially, for a contract to be binding, something of value must be exchanged.

Intention to Create Legal Relations

Case: Balfour v Balfour [1919] 2 KB 571

The Facts: A husband promised to pay his wife a monthly allowance while he was working abroad. When they separated, she sued for the money.

The Principle: The court held that agreements between spouses (domestic/social agreements) are presumed not to be legally binding. Unless there is clear evidence to the contrary, the law assumes parties in such relationships do not intend to create legal consequences.

Privity of Contract

Case: Dunlop Pneumatic Tyre Co Ltd v Selfridge & Co Ltd [1915] AC 847

The Principle: This case reinforced the doctrine of privity of contract, which states that a person who is not a party to a contract cannot sue or be sued under it. Only those who have provided consideration for a promise can enforce that promise. (Note: This has since been modified by the Contracts (Rights of Third Parties) Act 1999).

Terms of the Contract (Incorporation)

Case: Thornton v Shoe Lane Parking [1971] 2 QB 163

The Facts: Mr. Thornton parked in an automated car park. A sign inside said he was subject to conditions printed on the ticket. He didn't see the conditions until after he had paid.

The Principle: The court held that the conditions were not part of the contract because they were introduced after the contract was formed. Lord Denning famously noted that a customer cannot be bound by terms that they were not given a fair opportunity to see before the contract was concluded.

Frustration (Impossibility of Performance)

Case: Taylor v Caldwell (1863) 3 B & S 826

The Facts: A music hall was hired for a concert, but it burned down before the event.

The Principle: The court established the doctrine of frustration. If the subject matter of the contract is destroyed through no fault of either party, the contract is discharged, and neither party is liable for damages for failing to perform.

Misrepresentation

Case: Hedley Byrne & Co Ltd v Heller & Partners Ltd [1964] AC 465

The Principle: This case established the concept of negligent misstatement. It held that a person can be held liable for financial loss caused by a negligent statement, even in the absence of a contract, provided there is a "special relationship" between the parties where one relies on the expertise of the other.

Breach and Damages

Case: Hadley v Baxendale (1854) 9 Exch 341

The Principle: This is the leading case on the remoteness of damages. It established that a party in breach of contract is only liable for losses that were:

Naturally arising from the breach (the "normal" course of things).

In the reasonable contemplation of both parties at the time the contract was made (the "special" circumstances).

Conclusion

These landmark cases illustrate how judicial decisions have shaped breach of contract laws by clarifying essential principles such as offer and acceptance, consideration, damages, and enforcement mechanisms in both jurisdictions.

CHAPTER FIVE

UK and USA construction contract law and tort law principle

In both the UK and the USA, construction law is primarily governed by contract law (the agreement between parties). However, tort law (civil wrongs independent of contract) serves as a critical safety net, particularly when there is no direct contractual link between parties (e.g., between a homeowner and a subcontractor) or when a contract fails to cover specific damages.

While both jurisdictions share common law roots, they have diverged significantly in how they apply tort principles to construction.

1. The UK Approach: Narrowing the Scope

In the UK, the courts have historically been very restrictive about allowing tort claims in construction, primarily to protect the sanctity of the contract.

The "Economic Loss" Rule: The UK courts generally do not allow a party to recover "pure economic loss" (e.g., the cost of fixing a defect) in tort. Tort law is intended to protect against personal injury or damage to other property, not the quality of the building itself.

Negligence and Latent Defects: Following the landmark case Murphy v Brentwood District Council, the UK courts ruled that a builder is generally not liable in tort for the cost of repairing a defective building. If a building is defective, the owner must look to their contract (or a collateral warranty) for a remedy.

The Defective Premises Act 1972: Because tort law is so limited, the UK government created this statute to fill the gap. It imposes a statutory duty on those involved in building dwellings to ensure they are "fit for habitation." This acts as a "tort-like" remedy that exists outside of a direct contract.

Professional Negligence: Architects and engineers can be sued in tort for professional negligence if they breach their duty of care, provided the claimant can prove the professional failed to meet the standard of a reasonably competent professional.

2. The USA Approach: More Permissive but Complex

The US approach is fragmented because it is governed by individual state laws. However, generally, US courts are more willing than UK courts to allow tort claims in construction disputes.

The Economic Loss Doctrine: Like the UK, most US states have an "Economic Loss Rule." It prevents a party from suing in tort for purely financial losses (like repair costs) if those losses are better addressed by a contract. However, many states have significant exceptions.

Negligent Construction/Design: In many US jurisdictions, a contractor or architect can be sued for "negligent construction" or "negligent design" even by a party with whom they have no contract (e.g., a subsequent purchaser of a home). This is often framed as a breach of a "duty of care" to avoid creating a dangerous condition.

Third-Party Liability: In the US, it is common for subcontractors to be sued in tort by the project owner for negligence, even if there is no "privity of contract" between them. The courts often view the subcontractor as having a general duty to perform work in a "workmanlike manner."

Strict Liability: In some states, developers or builders of residential property can be held "strictly liable" for construction defects, meaning the plaintiff does not even need to prove negligence—only that the defect exists and caused damage.

The differences between UK and USA construction law are rooted in their respective legal systems: the UK operates under English Common Law (with a strong statutory overlay), while the USA operates under a decentralized state-based system where contract law varies significantly by jurisdiction.

Here are the key differences across five critical areas:

1. Statutory Adjudication (The "Security of Payment" Gap)

This is the most significant practical difference.

UK: The Housing Grants, Construction and Regeneration Act 1996 (the "Construction Act") introduced statutory adjudication. Any party to a construction contract has the right to refer a dispute to an independent adjudicator at any time. The decision is binding on an "interim" basis and must be complied with immediately, even if the party intends to take the matter to court or arbitration later. This provides a "pay now, argue later" mechanism that keeps cash flowing.

USA: There is no federal equivalent to the UK's statutory adjudication. While some states have "Prompt Payment Acts," they are often difficult to enforce without lengthy litigation or arbitration. Disputes are typically resolved through binding arbitration or litigation, which are slow and expensive, often leading to "pay when paid" or "pay if paid" clauses that can severely impact cash flow for subcontractors.

2. The Role of the "Contract Administrator"

UK: Standard forms (like the JCT) utilize an independent professional—the Contract Administrator or Architect—who acts as a certifier. They have a quasi-judicial duty to act impartially when certifying payments or granting extensions of time, even though they are paid by the employer.

USA: The role of the Architect/Engineer is generally limited to technical oversight. They are rarely given the power to act as an impartial certifier. Instead, the contract is viewed as a purely commercial arrangement between the Owner and the Contractor. If there is a dispute over payment or time, it is treated as a breach of contract claim rather than a failure of a certifier to perform their duty.

3. Liability and Negligence (Economic Loss)

UK: The law of tort (negligence) is generally restricted regarding "pure economic loss." If a contractor builds a defective building, the owner usually cannot sue in negligence for the cost of fixing it; they must sue under the contract. However, the UK has the Defective Premises Act 1972, which imposes a statutory duty on those involved in dwelling construction to ensure the work is fit for habitation.

USA: The "Economic Loss Rule" is a major feature of US law. It generally bars plaintiffs from recovering in tort for purely economic losses resulting from a contract breach. However, US courts are often more willing to find "negligent misrepresentation" or "professional malpractice" claims against architects and engineers, which can bypass some of the contractual limitations that exist in the UK.

4. Liquidated Damages (LDs) vs. Penalties

UK: The law on LDs has evolved significantly (notably the Cavendish Square case). An LD clause is enforceable if it protects a "legitimate interest" and is not "extravagant or unconscionable."

USA: US courts are historically stricter. An LD clause must be a reasonable forecast of actual damages at the time of contracting. If a court deems the LD amount to be a "penalty" (designed to punish the contractor rather than compensate the owner), it will be struck down, and the owner will be forced to prove their actual damages, which is often difficult and expensive.

5. Standard Forms of Contract

UK: The industry is dominated by a few highly standardized suites: JCT (Joint Contracts Tribunal) for building works and NEC (New Engineering Contract) for infrastructure. These are widely understood, and there is a massive body of case law interpreting them.

USA: While the AIA (American Institute of Architects) and ConsensusDocs forms are popular, they are frequently heavily amended. Because US law varies by state, "standard" forms are often customized to comply with local lien laws, indemnity statutes, and insurance requirements, making every contract unique and harder to interpret through precedent.

The intersection of construction contract law and tort law is a complex area, primarily because construction projects involve a web of contractual relationships (the "contractual matrix") that courts are often reluctant to disturb with tortious duties.

Below is an analysis of the key principles and landmark cases in both the UK and the USA.

1. The UK Perspective: The "Contractual Matrix"

In the UK, the courts generally prioritize the sanctity of the contract. If a contract exists, the parties are expected to rely on their contractual remedies rather than tort law (negligence).

Key Principles:

Economic Loss: English law generally prohibits the recovery of "pure economic loss" in tort (e.g., the cost of fixing a defective building that hasn't caused physical injury).

Assumption of Responsibility: For a duty of care to exist in tort between parties without a direct contract (e.g., an owner and a sub-contractor), the claimant must prove the defendant "assumed responsibility" for the claimant's economic welfare.

The Defective Premises Act 1972: This provides a statutory route for claims regarding defective dwellings, bypassing some common law hurdles.

Landmark Cases:

Junior Books Ltd v Veitchi Co Ltd [1983]: An outlier case where the House of Lords allowed a building owner to sue a sub-contractor in tort for defective flooring. It is rarely followed today and is considered an anomaly.

Murphy v Brentwood District Council [1991]: The definitive case that overruled Anns v Merton. It established that a local authority is not liable in tort for the cost of repairing a defective building, reinforcing the "pure economic loss" bar.

Robinson v PE Jones (Contractors) Ltd [2011]: Confirmed that a contractor does not owe a concurrent duty of care in tort that is broader than their contractual obligations.

2. The USA Perspective: The "Economic Loss Rule"

In the US, the "Economic Loss Rule" (ELR) is the dominant doctrine. It prevents a party from recovering in tort for purely economic losses that arise from a breach of contract.

Key Principles:

The Economic Loss Rule: If the damage is to the "product itself" (the building) and not to other property or people, the claimant is limited to contract remedies (warranty/breach of contract).

Privity of Contract: In many US jurisdictions, you cannot sue a party for negligence if you do not have a contract with them (lack of privity), unless there is a specific exception (e.g., professional malpractice).

Professional Liability: Architects and engineers are often held to a "professional standard of care," which can sometimes be litigated in tort, even if the underlying relationship is contractual.

Landmark Cases:

East River Steamship Corp. v. Transamerica Delaval, Inc. (1986): A US Supreme Court case that solidified the Economic Loss Rule in maritime law, which has since been adopted by almost every state in construction litigation. It held that when a product injures only itself, the remedy is in contract (warranty), not tort.

Berschauer/Phillips Construction Co. v. Seattle School District (1994): A Washington State case that is frequently cited. It held that a general contractor could not sue the project architect for negligence because the contractor's losses were purely economic and governed by the construction contract.

3. Comparative Analysis: Key Differences

FeatureUK ApproachUSA Approach

Pure Economic LossGenerally barred, but "Assumption of Responsibility" can create exceptions.Strictly barred under the Economic Loss Rule.

Concurrent LiabilityPossible to have both contract and tort claims, but tort cannot expand contract scope.Generally prohibited by the Economic Loss Rule; contract is the exclusive remedy.

Third-Party ClaimsContracts (Rights of Third Parties) Act 1999 allows third parties to enforce contracts.Strict adherence to privity; third-party beneficiaries must be explicitly named.

Professional NegligenceArchitects/Engineers owe a duty of care in tort regardless of contract.Often treated as a breach of contract unless specific state statutes allow tort claims.

4. Practical Implications for Construction Law

The "Chain of Contracts": In both jurisdictions, the preferred method of risk allocation is through the contract (e.g., collateral warranties in the UK, or indemnity clauses in the US). Courts prefer that parties "contract around" the risks rather than relying on tort law.

Limitation Periods: Tort law often has different limitation periods (statutes of limitations) than contract law. Claimants often try to plead tort to bypass the shorter limitation periods found in construction contracts.

Insurance: Tort claims are often covered by Professional Indemnity (PI) insurance, whereas contract claims may be covered by different policies. This is often the hidden driver behind why lawyers attempt to frame a case as "negligence" rather than "breach of contract."

Conclusion

If you are dealing with a construction dispute:

In the UK: Look for an "assumption of responsibility" or a breach of the Defective Premises Act.

In the USA: Look for exceptions to the Economic Loss Rule (e.g., fraud, negligent misrepresentation, or damage to "other property") to move the case out of the contract box and into the tort box.

1. United Kingdom: The Statutory Framework

The UK construction industry is heavily regulated by specific legislation designed to ensure cash flow and fair payment practices.

Key Legislation:

The Housing Grants, Construction and Regeneration Act 1996 (The "Construction Act"): This is the cornerstone of UK construction law. It mandates:

Adjudication: A statutory right for parties to refer disputes to an independent adjudicator at any time. This provides a "pay now, argue later" mechanism.

Payment Provisions: It dictates how payments must be made, requiring clear "payment notices" and "pay-less notices" to prevent unfair withholding of funds.

The Scheme for Construction Contracts: If a contract does not comply with the Construction Act, the "Scheme" is automatically implied into the contract to fill the gaps regarding payment and adjudication.

Standard Forms of Contract:

Unlike the US, the UK relies heavily on standardized, industry-wide contract suites:

JCT (Joint Contracts Tribunal): The most common form for building works.

NEC (New Engineering Contract): Focuses on collaborative project management and risk sharing; widely used in public sector and infrastructure projects.

FIDIC: Often used for international projects, but also utilized in large-scale UK infrastructure.

2. United States: The Contractual/Common Law Framework

The US does not have a single federal "Construction Act." Instead, construction law is a patchwork of state-level statutes, common law, and private contract law.

Key Frameworks:

State Law: Construction law is primarily governed by the state where the project is located. This includes state-specific Mechanics Lien laws (which allow contractors to place a lien on a property if they aren't paid) and Prompt Payment Acts (which vary significantly by state).

Common Law: Contract interpretation, breach of contract, and negligence claims are governed by state common law and the Uniform Commercial Code (UCC) (though the UCC primarily applies to the sale of goods, it is often applied to construction materials).

Licensing Laws: Every state has strict licensing requirements for contractors. Operating without a license can often render a contract unenforceable.

Standard Forms of Contract:

AIA (American Institute of Architects): The industry standard in the US. The AIA documents (e.g., A101, A201) are widely used and have been tested by decades of litigation, making them highly predictable for courts.

ConsensusDocs: A coalition-based alternative to AIA, often favored by contractors because it is perceived as more balanced between the owner, contractor, and architect.

DBIA (Design-Build Institute of America): Specifically used for design-build delivery methods.

The legal frameworks governing construction contracts and torts in the UK and the USA differ significantly due to their respective legal systems (Common Law vs. Civil/Statutory nuances) and the way they allocate risk.

Below is an overview of the main frameworks in both jurisdictions.

1. The United Kingdom

The UK operates under a "Common Law" system, heavily influenced by freedom of contract, but increasingly regulated by statutory interventions to protect sub-contractors and ensure payment.

A. Construction Contracts

The Housing Grants, Construction and Regeneration Act 1996 (The "Construction Act"): This is the primary legislation. It mandates the right to adjudication (a fast-track dispute resolution process) and sets out strict rules regarding payment notices to prevent "pay-when-paid" clauses.

Standard Forms of Contract: Unlike the US, the UK construction industry relies heavily on standardized, industry-vetted contracts:

JCT (Joint Contracts Tribunal): The most common for building works.

NEC (New Engineering Contract): Focuses on collaborative project management; widely used in public infrastructure.

FIDIC: Used for international projects.

The Defective Premises Act 1972: Imposes a statutory duty on those involved in building dwellings to ensure they are "fit for habitation."

B. Tort Law

Negligence: The primary tort in construction. Contractors owe a duty of care to third parties (e.g., future owners) if their work creates a danger to health and safety.

Nuisance: Often invoked in construction disputes regarding noise, dust, vibration, or interference with neighboring land.

Economic Loss: UK law is generally restrictive regarding "pure economic loss" in tort. You generally cannot sue in tort for the cost of fixing a defective building; you must rely on the contract.

2. The United States

The US system is decentralized. While there are federal regulations for government projects, most construction law is governed by State Law.

A. Construction Contracts

Freedom of Contract: US courts generally uphold the "four corners" of the contract. There is no federal equivalent to the UK's "Construction Act" that mandates adjudication; however, many states have "Prompt Payment Acts" that regulate payment timelines.

Standard Forms of Contract:

AIA (American Institute of Architects): The industry standard for private commercial projects.

ConsensusDocs: A coalition-based alternative to AIA.

FAR (Federal Acquisition Regulation): Governs all US federal government construction projects.

Mechanic's Liens: A critical statutory framework in every state. It allows contractors and suppliers to place a lien on the property if they are not paid, effectively clouding the title until the debt is settled.

B. Tort Law

Negligence: Similar to the UK, but with a major distinction: the "Economic Loss Rule."

In most US states, if a contractor performs defective work, the owner cannot sue in tort for the cost of the repair. They are limited to contract remedies (breach of contract/warranty). Tort is reserved for cases involving physical injury or damage to other property.

Strict Liability: In some states, developers/builders can be held strictly liable for construction defects that cause property damage or personal injury, regardless of fault.

Professional Malpractice: Architects and engineers are held to a "standard of care" in tort, which can be litigated independently of the contract.

CHAPTER SIX

UK and USA construction contract law and tort law cases questions

Negligence claims are a significant source of legal and financial risk in the construction industries of both the UK and the USA. While both jurisdictions share a common law heritage, the mechanisms for handling these claims and the resulting impacts on projects differ in nuance and practice.

Here is an analysis of how negligence claims affect construction projects in both regions.

1. The Core Impact: "The Project Chill"

In both countries, the threat of negligence litigation creates a "defensive" project culture.

Increased Costs: To mitigate risk, contractors and consultants often build "risk premiums" into their bids.

Documentation Burden: Projects become bogged down in excessive record-keeping. While this is good for accountability, it often slows down decision-making and increases administrative overhead.

Insurance Premiums: Professional Indemnity (PI) insurance costs are a major overhead. High-profile negligence cases often lead to "hard markets" where insurance becomes prohibitively expensive, potentially forcing smaller firms out of the market.

2. The UK Context: Contractual Primacy

In the UK, the courts are generally reluctant to allow negligence claims if a contract already exists between the parties.

The "Contractual Shield": UK courts prefer to look at the contract to determine liability. If a contractor fails to perform, the remedy is usually a breach of contract claim, not negligence. Negligence is typically reserved for cases involving personal injury or damage to property outside the scope of the contract.

Economic Loss: A major hurdle in the UK is the recovery of "pure economic loss" (e.g., the cost of fixing a defect that hasn't caused physical damage yet). The UK courts (following Murphy v Brentwood) are very restrictive here, meaning negligence claims for "shoddy work" that hasn't caused an accident are difficult to sustain.

The Building Safety Act 2022: This is a game-changer in the UK. It extends the limitation period for claims regarding defective dwellings to 30 years (retrospectively) and 15 years (prospectively). This has created a massive surge in negligence-related litigation concerning fire safety and cladding.

3. The USA Context: Tort and "Economic Loss Rule"

In the US, the construction industry is highly litigious, and the interaction between contract law and tort law (negligence) is more complex.

The Economic Loss Rule (ELR): Similar to the UK, most US states apply the ELR, which prevents a party from suing in tort (negligence) if the loss is purely financial (e.g., the building is worth less than expected). However, there are many state-specific exceptions, making the legal landscape unpredictable.

Professional Negligence (Malpractice): Architects and engineers are held to a "standard of care." If they fail to meet the standard of a reasonably prudent professional in their field, they can be sued for negligence. This often leads to "blame-shifting" during construction disputes, where the owner sues the architect, who then sues the contractor, and vice versa.

Third-Party Liability: US law is often more permissive regarding third-party negligence claims. If a design defect causes a building to collapse, the architect may be held liable for negligence to parties they have no direct contract with (e.g., future tenants or the public), which is much harder to achieve in the UK.

4. Key Differences in Project Impact

FeatureUnited KingdomUnited States

Primary FocusContractual remedies (Breach of Contract).Tort-based remedies (Negligence/Professional Malpractice).

Economic LossVery difficult to recover in negligence.Varies by state; often barred but with many exceptions.

Limitation PeriodsGenerally 6–12 years; 30 years for building safety.Varies by state; often tied to "statutes of repose" (e.g., 10 years).

Dispute ResolutionStrong emphasis on Adjudication (fast, interim).Heavy reliance on litigation and arbitration.

1. In both the UK and the USA, a construction fatality caused by an engineer's negligence triggers two distinct legal tracks: Criminal Law (state/government prosecution) and Civil Tort Law (lawsuits for damages). If an engineer neglects construction safety processes, leading to a worker's death, here is how the legal systems generally handle it.

1. The UK Legal Framework

The UK has very strict health and safety laws. The engineer would likely face scrutiny under the Health and Safety at Work etc. Act 1974.

Criminal Liability: The Health and Safety Executive (HSE) would investigate. If the engineer's failure to consider the construction process was a "gross breach" of their duty of care, they could be charged with Gross Negligence Manslaughter. This can lead to significant prison time.

Civil Tort Liability: The family of the deceased would sue the engineer (or more commonly, their employer/firm) for "Wrongful Death" or "Negligence."

Duty of Care: The court would establish that the engineer owed a duty of care to the workers on-site.

Breach: The court would look at the "Bolam Test" or "Bolitho Test"—would a responsible body of engineers have ignored the construction process in the same way? If the answer is no, the engineer is found negligent.

Causation: The plaintiff must prove that the engineer's specific neglect was the direct cause of the death.

2. The USA Legal Framework

In the USA, the process is heavily focused on state-level tort law and federal safety regulations (OSHA).

OSHA (Federal): The Occupational Safety and Health Administration would investigate. While OSHA primarily fines companies, if the negligence was willful and resulted in death, the Department of Justice can pursue criminal charges against individuals.

Civil Tort Liability (Negligence/Wrongful Death): The family would file a civil lawsuit against the engineer and the firm.

Professional Malpractice: Because the engineer is a licensed professional, the lawsuit would be framed as "Professional Negligence." The court would look at the "Standard of Care"—what would a reasonably prudent engineer have done under similar circumstances?

Vicarious Liability: In the US, the firm is usually sued alongside the engineer under the doctrine of Respondeat Superior (the employer is responsible for the acts of the employee). The firm usually has the "deep pockets" (insurance) to pay the damages.

Comparative Negligence: The defense will often try to argue that the worker or the construction contractor also contributed to the accident. The court will assign a percentage of fault to each party.

How the Court Determines "Neglect"

In both jurisdictions, a judge or jury will look for the following to determine if the engineer is liable:

Foreseeability: Could the engineer have reasonably foreseen that failing to plan for the construction process would create a lethal hazard?

Professional Standards: Did the engineer violate industry codes (such as the American Society of Civil Engineers (ASCE) Code of Ethics or the UK's Construction (Design and Management) Regulations - CDM 2015)?

Proximate Cause: Was the death a direct result of the engineer's failure to design a safe process, or was it caused by a contractor ignoring the engineer's instructions?

The Reality of "Who Gets Sued"

In practice, it is rare for an individual engineer to be sued personally for the full amount of a wrongful death claim. Instead:

The Firm is Sued: The firm carries Professional Indemnity Insurance (UK) or Errors and Omissions (E&O) Insurance (USA). The insurance company handles the defense and pays the settlement.

Licensing Boards: Beyond the court, the engineer's professional license (PE in the USA, CEng in the UK) would likely be reviewed by a regulatory board. They could be stripped of their license, effectively ending their career.

Case analysis 1

In both the UK and the USA, if an engineer causes their employer to lose money by failing to read or sign a contract properly, the legal framework for holding them accountable is generally Contract Law (Employment Law) rather than Tort Law.

The breakdown of how these systems view such a situation:

1. The Primary Path: Contract Law (Breach of Employment Contract)

In both the UK and the USA, the relationship between an engineer and their employer is governed by an Employment Contract.

Duty of Care/Performance: Every employment contract contains an implied (or explicit) term that the employee will perform their duties with "reasonable care and skill."

Breach: If an engineer is tasked with reviewing and signing a contract and fails to read it—thereby causing financial loss—they have failed to perform their professional duties to the standard expected of their role.

The Result: The employer would sue the engineer for breach of contract. The employer would argue that the engineer's negligence in their professional duties resulted in a direct financial loss to the firm.

2. Why Tort Law is Less Likely

"Tort" refers to a civil wrong (like negligence) that causes harm. While the engineer's actions were "negligent" in the common sense, courts generally prefer to handle these issues through Contract Law for the following reasons:

The "Economic Loss Rule": In many US states and under UK common law, you generally cannot sue for "pure economic loss" in tort if a contract already exists between the parties. The courts take the view that the employment contract is the "master" document that defines the responsibilities and liabilities of both parties.

Contractual Allocation of Risk: Courts prefer to look at what the employment contract says about liability. If the contract doesn't mention liability for negligence, the court will apply the standard of the "reasonable employee."

3. Key Differences: UK vs. USA

In the UK:

Vicarious Liability: If the engineer's mistake caused the firm to lose money to a third party (e.g., a client), the firm is usually held "vicariously liable" for the engineer's mistake. The firm can then seek to recover those losses from the engineer, but this is often difficult unless the engineer was grossly negligent or acted in bad faith.

Employment Rights: UK employment law is very protective of employees. Unless the engineer's contract specifically outlines financial penalties for negligence, it is often difficult for an employer to sue an employee for damages unless the conduct was willful or reckless.

In the USA:

At-Will Employment: In most US states, employment is "at-will." While an employer can fire an engineer for this mistake, suing an employee for financial damages is rarer than in other countries.

Indemnification: Many US employment contracts include clauses where the employee agrees to indemnify the employer for losses caused by their gross negligence. However, courts often scrutinize these clauses to ensure they aren't unconscionable.

Professional Liability (Errors & Omissions): If the engineer is a licensed Professional Engineer (PE), the firm likely carries "Errors and Omissions" (E&O) insurance. The insurance company usually covers the loss, and they may choose to terminate the engineer rather than sue them, as suing an employee is often seen as bad for morale and expensive.

4. What would a court look for?

Regardless of whether it is framed as a contract or tort claim, the court will look at:

Scope of Duty: Was it actually the engineer's job to read and sign that contract? Did they have the authority to do so?

Standard of Care: Did the engineer act as a "reasonably competent engineer" would have in the same situation?

Causation: Did the failure to read the contract directly cause the financial loss, or was the loss caused by other market factors?

Mitigation: Did the employer have a system in place to double-check the engineer's work? (If the firm failed to have a review process, they may be found partially liable for their own loss).

Summary

If an engineer causes a loss due to negligence, the employer's primary recourse is Breach of Contract. However, in practice, employers usually fire the employee rather than sue them. Suing an employee is costly, and the employee often lacks the personal assets to cover a large construction-related financial loss, making a lawsuit a poor way for a firm to recover money.

Case analysis 2

In both the UK and the USA, a construction fatality caused by an engineer's negligence triggers two distinct legal tracks: Criminal Law (state/government prosecution) and Civil Tort Law (lawsuits for damages). If an engineer neglects construction safety processes, leading to a worker's death, here is how the legal systems generally handle it.

1. The UK Legal Framework

The UK has very strict health and safety laws. The engineer would likely face scrutiny under the Health and Safety at Work etc. Act 1974.

Criminal Liability: The Health and Safety Executive (HSE) would investigate. If the engineer's failure to consider the construction process was a "gross breach" of their duty of care, they could be charged with Gross Negligence Manslaughter. This can lead to significant prison time.

Civil Tort Liability: The family of the deceased would sue the engineer (or more commonly, their employer/firm) for "Wrongful Death" or "Negligence."

Duty of Care: The court would establish that the engineer owed a duty of care to the workers on-site.

Breach: The court would look at the "Bolam Test" or "Bolitho Test"—would a responsible body of engineers have ignored the construction process in the same way? If the answer is no, the engineer is found negligent.

Causation: The plaintiff must prove that the engineer's specific neglect was the direct cause of the death.

2. The USA Legal Framework

In the USA, the process is heavily focused on state-level tort law and federal safety regulations (OSHA).

OSHA (Federal): The Occupational Safety and Health Administration would investigate. While OSHA primarily fines companies, if the negligence was willful and resulted in death, the Department of Justice can pursue criminal charges against individuals.

Civil Tort Liability (Negligence/Wrongful Death): The family would file a civil lawsuit against the engineer and the firm.

Professional Malpractice: Because the engineer is a licensed professional, the lawsuit would be framed as "Professional Negligence." The court would look at the "Standard of Care"—what would a reasonably prudent engineer have done under similar circumstances?

Vicarious Liability: In the US, the firm is usually sued alongside the engineer under the doctrine of Respondeat Superior (the employer is responsible for the acts of the employee). The firm usually has the "deep pockets" (insurance) to pay the damages.

Comparative Negligence: The defense will often try to argue that the worker or the construction contractor also contributed to the accident. The court will assign a percentage of fault to each party.

How the Court Determines "Neglect"

In both jurisdictions, a judge or jury will look for the following to determine if the engineer is liable:

Foreseeability: Could the engineer have reasonably foreseen that failing to plan for the construction process would create a lethal hazard?

Professional Standards: Did the engineer violate industry codes (such as the American Society of Civil Engineers (ASCE) Code of Ethics or the UK's Construction (Design and Management) Regulations - CDM 2015)?

Proximate Cause: Was the death a direct result of the engineer's failure to design a safe process, or was it caused by a contractor ignoring the engineer's instructions?

The Reality of "Who Gets Sued"

In practice, it is rare for an individual engineer to be sued personally for the full amount of a wrongful death claim. Instead:

The Firm is Sued: The firm carries Professional Indemnity Insurance (UK) or Errors and Omissions (E&O) Insurance (USA). The insurance company handles the defense and pays the settlement.

Licensing Boards: Beyond the court, the engineer's professional license (PE in the USA, CEng in the UK) would likely be reviewed by a regulatory board. They could be stripped of their license, effectively ending their career.

Summary

If an engineer neglects the construction process and a worker dies:

Criminal courts may imprison the engineer for gross negligence or manslaughter.

Civil courts will order the engineer's firm to pay massive financial damages to the worker's family.

Regulatory bodies will likely revoke the engineer's professional license.

Case analysis 3

In both the United States and the United Kingdom, the legal situation you described involves a complex interplay between Employment Law and Tort Law. If two workers cause a fire through carelessness (negligence) and have no money to pay for the damages, the legal system generally approaches the situation in the following way:

In both the United States and the United Kingdom, tort law serves as the primary mechanism for addressing negligence in construction. While the core principles—duty, breach, causation, and damages—are similar, the legal frameworks, procedural nuances, and approaches to economic loss differ significantly.USA and UK construction contract and tort law principle as below:

1. The Core Framework: The "Four Pillars"

In both jurisdictions, a plaintiff (claimant) must prove four elements to succeed in a negligence claim:

Duty of Care: The defendant owed a legal obligation to the plaintiff to act with reasonable care.

Breach: The defendant failed to meet the standard of care expected of a "reasonably competent" professional or contractor.

Causation: The breach directly caused the injury or damage (factual and legal causation).

Damages: The plaintiff suffered actual, quantifiable harm (personal injury, property damage, or, in some cases, economic loss).

2. The United Kingdom: The "Contract-Tort" Divide

In the UK, construction law is heavily influenced by the Law of Contract. Because most construction projects are governed by complex, multi-tiered contracts (e.g., JCT or NEC forms), the courts prefer to resolve disputes through contract law rather than tort.

The "Pure Economic Loss" Barrier: UK courts are historically reluctant to allow tort claims for "pure economic loss" (e.g., the cost of fixing a defect that hasn't caused physical injury). If a building is poorly constructed but hasn't collapsed or hurt anyone, the owner usually must sue under contract law (breach of warranty).

The Defective Premises Act 1972: This is a crucial statutory exception. It imposes a duty on those involved in building dwellings to ensure they are fit for habitation. It allows claimants to bypass some common law restrictions on tort claims.

Professional Negligence: Architects and engineers are held to the Bolam test (or Bolitho refinement), which asks whether the professional acted in accordance with a practice accepted as proper by a responsible body of professional opinion.

3. The United States: The "Economic Loss Rule"

In the US, construction negligence is governed by state common law, leading to significant variation between states.

The Economic Loss Rule (ELR): This is the most significant hurdle in US construction torts. Most states bar plaintiffs from recovering in tort for purely economic losses (e.g., the cost of repairing a defective wall) if there is no accompanying personal injury or damage to "other property." The rationale is that the parties should have allocated these risks in their contract.

Negligent Misrepresentation: To circumvent the ELR, US plaintiffs often sue architects or engineers for "negligent misrepresentation." If a professional provides faulty plans that lead to increased construction costs, the plaintiff may argue the professional provided false information upon which they reasonably relied.

Third-Party Liability: In the US, a major area of tort litigation involves "General Contractor liability" for the safety of subcontractors' employees. Under the Restatement (Second) of Torts § 414, if a general contractor retains "control" over the work, they may be held liable for the negligence of a subcontractor.

4. Key Differences at a Glance

FeatureUnited KingdomUnited States

Primary DriverContract law dominates; tort is a "gap-filler."Contract law dominates; tort is often barred by ELR.

Economic LossGenerally barred in tort (with exceptions).Strictly barred by the Economic Loss Rule.

Safety StandardsHeavily regulated by statutory health and safety laws (CDM Regulations).Heavily regulated by OSHA and state-specific building codes.

Professional StandardBolam test (peer-based standard)."Reasonable professional" standard (often expert testimony).

This construction site two employees cause fire accident case law analysis steps as below:

1. Vicarious Liability (The Employer's Burden)

In both the US and the UK, there is a legal doctrine called Vicarious Liability. This means that an employer is generally held legally responsible for the negligent acts of their employees, provided those acts occurred "within the scope of their employment."

The Result: If the workers were doing their jobs (even if they were doing them carelessly) when the fire started, the building owner will likely sue the construction company, not the individual workers.

Why? The company is considered to have "deep pockets" (insurance and assets), whereas the workers do not. The law assumes that the risk of employee negligence is a cost of doing business.

2. Suing the Employees Directly (Tort Law)

While the employer is usually the target, the construction company (or their insurance provider) could technically sue the individual workers for negligence (a Tort).

In the UK: Under the Civil Liability (Contribution) Act 1978 and general common law, an employer can seek an "indemnity" or contribution from an employee. However, in practice, this is extremely rare. Most employment contracts include "indemnity clauses" that protect employees from being personally liable for accidents unless the damage was caused by gross misconduct or willful/malicious intent (e.g., they set the fire on purpose).

In the US: Similar to the UK, employers rarely sue their own employees for simple negligence. If they did, the employee would be liable under Tort law. However, if the employee has no money, a "judgment" against them is essentially worthless. You cannot get blood from a stone; if the worker has no assets, the company cannot collect the money.

3. The "No Money" Problem (Judgment Proof)

If the court finds the workers liable, but they have no money, they are considered "judgment proof."

The court will issue a judgment, but the employer will never be able to collect the money.

This is why employers rely on Commercial General Liability (CGL) insurance. The insurance company pays for the damage caused by the employees' negligence, and the insurance company usually waives the right to sue the employees because it is not cost-effective.

4. What if they hide the truth?

You mentioned that the workers "do not talk" about being the cause.

Investigation: In both the US and UK, insurance companies will conduct a forensic investigation (fire marshals, electrical experts, etc.) to determine the cause of the fire. They do not need the workers to confess to prove negligence.

Termination: If the employer discovers the workers were responsible and were lying about it, this is usually grounds for "summary dismissal" (firing for cause). In the UK, this would be "gross misconduct." In the US, this would be "termination for cause," which would likely disqualify them from unemployment benefits.

5. Criminal Liability

If the carelessness was extreme (e.g., smoking in a restricted area, ignoring safety protocols, or violating fire codes), this moves from Tort Law (civil) to Criminal Law. The workers could be charged with arson (if intentional) or criminal negligence/endangerment (if reckless). If convicted, they could face fines or prison time. However, this still does not help the employer get their money back; it is a punishment by the state.

Summary

Who gets sued? The employer (the construction company) is sued by the building owner.

Can the employer sue the workers? Legally, yes (Tort law), but practically, no. They have no money, and employment contracts often protect workers from simple negligence.

What happens to the workers? They will likely be fired for cause. If the fire was caused by a violation of safety laws, they could face criminal charges.

Case analysis 4

CHAPTER SEVEN

UK and USA movie producer contract law and tort law cases questions

Copyright laws in the United States and the United Kingdom are governed by international treaties (such as the Berne Convention), meaning they are remarkably similar in practice. However, there are nuances in how they are enforced and interpreted.

How copyright applies to story content in both jurisdictions.

1. The Core Principle: "Idea vs. Expression"

In both the US and the UK, copyright does not protect ideas, themes, plots, or historical facts.

What is protected: The specific expression of the story (the actual words, the unique sequence of events, the specific dialogue, and the unique character development).

What is NOT protected: The "stock" elements of a story. You cannot copyright the idea of a "boy wizard," a "detective solving a murder," or a "dystopian government." These are known as scènes à faire—elements that are standard to a genre.

2. The United States (Copyright Act of 1976)

Automatic Protection: Copyright exists the moment a story is "fixed in a tangible medium" (written down or recorded). You do not need to register it to own the copyright.

Registration: While automatic, you must register your work with the U.S. Copyright Office if you want to sue for statutory damages or attorney's fees in federal court.

Duration: For works created by an individual, the term is the life of the author plus 70 years.

Fair Use: The US has a broad "Fair Use" doctrine (Section 107). It allows for the use of copyrighted material without permission for purposes like criticism, comment, news reporting, teaching, or research, based on a four-factor balancing test.

3. The United Kingdom (Copyright, Designs and Patents Act 1988)

Automatic Protection: Similar to the US, copyright is automatic upon creation. There is no formal registration system for copyright in the UK.

Duration: Generally, the term is the life of the author plus 70 years.

Fair Dealing: The UK does not have "Fair Use." Instead, it has "Fair Dealing." This is much narrower than the US version. It only applies to specific categories (e.g., private study, research, criticism, review, or news reporting). If your use doesn't fall into one of these specific "buckets," it is likely copyright infringement, regardless of how "fair" it seems.

Moral Rights: The UK places a stronger emphasis on "Moral Rights." Even if an author sells the copyright to a publisher, they retain the right to be identified as the author (paternity right) and the right to object to derogatory treatment of their work (integrity right).

4. Key Differences to Note

FeatureUnited StatesUnited Kingdom

RegistrationOptional, but required for lawsuits.None exists.

Exceptions"Fair Use" (Broad/Flexible)."Fair Dealing" (Narrow/Specific).

Moral RightsLimited (mostly for visual arts).Stronger (applies to literary works).

Work for HireEmployer is the legal author.Employee is the author (unless contract states otherwise).

5. Common Pitfalls for Writers

Fan Fiction: Technically, writing fan fiction is a copyright infringement because it uses protected characters and settings without permission. However, most copyright holders tolerate it because it acts as free marketing. If you try to sell fan fiction, you are almost certainly infringing on the original author's rights.

Plagiarism vs. Copyright Infringement: Plagiarism is an ethical/academic issue (claiming someone else's work as your own). Copyright infringement is a legal issue (using someone else's protected expression without permission). You can be guilty of one without the other.

Public Domain: Once the copyright expires (life + 70 years), the work enters the public domain. You are then free to use the characters, plot, and text however you wish (e.g., Sherlock Holmes or Pride and Prejudice).

Summary Advice

Originality is key: If you write your own story, you own the copyright.

Don't copy expression: You can write a story about a wizard, but don't name him Harry, don't give him a lightning bolt scar, and don't send him to a school called Hogwarts.

Consult a professional: If you are planning to adapt someone else's work or are worried about a potential infringement, consult an intellectual property (IP) attorney.

In both the USA and the UK, using another producer's story content without permission is a serious legal risk. While copyright law protects the expression of an idea rather than the idea itself, the line between "inspiration" and "infringement" is often litigated.

The legal implications in both jurisdictions.

1. Copyright Infringement

Copyright protects original works of authorship fixed in a tangible medium (scripts, treatments, novels).

The "Substantial Similarity" Test: To win a lawsuit, the original creator must prove that the second producer had access to the work and that the two works are "substantially similar."

Expression vs. Idea: You cannot copyright a generic plot (e.g., "a hero goes on a journey"). However, you can copyright the specific sequence of events, dialogue, character development, and unique world-building. If a producer copies the "total concept and feel" of a script, they are liable for infringement.

Consequences:

Injunctions: A court can issue an immediate "cease and desist" or an injunction, effectively killing the production and preventing the film from being released.

Statutory Damages: In the US, if the work was registered with the Copyright Office, the plaintiff can seek statutory damages (up to $150,000 per work for willful infringement) plus attorney's fees.

Actual Damages/Profits: The plaintiff can sue for the profits the infringing film made, which can be catastrophic for a production company.

2. Breach of Implied Contract (The "Idea Theft" Claim)

In the US (particularly in California), producers are often sued under the theory of "Implied-in-Fact Contract" (often called a Desny claim).

The Scenario: If a writer submits a script or pitch to a producer with the expectation of being paid, and the producer uses that material without payment, the law may imply a contract existed.

The Implication: Even if the material wasn't strictly copyrightable (e.g., just a "pitch"), the producer can be held liable for the value of the idea if they accepted the pitch under circumstances where payment was implied.

3. Breach of Confidence (UK Law)

In the UK, the concept of "Breach of Confidence" is a powerful tool for creators.

The Doctrine: If a creator shares a story with a producer in a confidential setting (e.g., a pitch meeting or an email marked "confidential"), the producer has a legal obligation not to use that information for their own benefit.

The Implication: If the producer uses the story, they can be sued for breach of confidence, even if the work hasn't been formally copyrighted or published.

4. Moral Rights (UK/EU focus)

The UK (via the Copyright, Designs and Patents Act 1988) recognizes "Moral Rights," which are stronger than those in the US.

Right of Paternity: The right to be identified as the author.

Right of Integrity: The right to object to "derogatory treatment" of the work.

If a producer takes a story and changes it in a way that the original author finds offensive or damaging to their reputation, the producer could face litigation based on these moral rights.

5. Practical/Industry Consequences

Beyond the courtroom, the professional fallout is often just as damaging:

Errors and Omissions (E&O) Insurance: No reputable distributor or streaming platform (Netflix, Amazon, etc.) will distribute a film without E&O insurance. If an insurer discovers that a producer used unauthorized content, they will refuse to cover the film, effectively making the film unmarketable.

"Blacklisting": The film industry is small. Producers known for "stealing" ideas are often shunned by agents, managers, and talent, making it impossible to secure future financing or cast.

Chain of Title Issues: To sell a film, a producer must prove a clean "chain of title" (legal documentation showing they own all rights to the story). If the chain is broken by a claim of theft, the film's value drops to zero.

Summary of Differences

USA: Heavily reliant on Copyright Law and Implied Contract claims. Litigation is expensive and aggressive.

UK: Relies on Copyright and the Equitable Doctrine of Breach of Confidence. The courts are generally less prone to massive jury awards than in the US, but the legal costs and the risk of an injunction remain high.

This scenario involves complex issues of Intellectual Property (IP) law (Copyright) rather than just general contract or tort law. In both the USA and the UK, the legal system protects original creative expression.

Case analysis 1

This case explains how a court in the USA or UK would analyze a situation where Producer A claims Producer B copied 15 minutes of their story.

1. The Core Legal Issue: Copyright Infringement

In both jurisdictions, you cannot sue for "stealing a story" unless that story is protected by copyright.

Idea vs. Expression: Copyright law protects the expression of an idea (the specific script, dialogue, scenes, and character development), but it does not protect the idea itself (e.g., "a story about a boy who goes to wizard school").

Substantial Similarity: For Producer A to sue Producer B, they must prove that Producer B's 15 minutes are "substantially similar" to Producer A's protected work. If Producer B only took a generic plot point, they might not be liable. If they copied specific dialogue, unique plot twists, or distinct character arcs, they are likely infringing.

2. Can Producer A sue under Contract Law?

Generally, no.

Contract law requires a pre-existing agreement (a contract) between the two parties.

If Producer A and Producer B never signed a contract, never had a meeting, and never entered into a non-disclosure agreement (NDA), there is no contract to breach. You cannot sue someone for "breach of contract" if no contract exists.

3. Can Producer A sue under Tort Law?

In the context of movie production, "tort" claims are usually limited.

Copyright Infringement is a Statutory Tort: In both the UK and USA, copyright infringement is treated as a civil wrong (a tort). Producer A would sue under the Copyright Act (USA) or the Copyright, Designs and Patents Act 1988 (UK).

"Passing Off" (UK) or "Unfair Competition" (USA): If Producer B is trying to trick the audience into thinking their movie is actually Producer A's movie (e.g., using similar branding or titles), Producer A might sue for "Passing Off" (UK) or "Unfair Competition/False Designation of Origin" (USA). This is a tort claim.

4. Compensation for Profit Loss

If Producer A successfully proves that Producer B infringed on their copyright, the court can award damages. These usually come in two forms:

Actual Damages: The money Producer A lost because the audience watched Producer B's movie instead of theirs.

Disgorgement of Profits: The court may order Producer B to hand over the profits they made specifically from the 15 minutes of copied content.

5. The "15 Minutes out of 120 minutes" Defense

Producer B will likely argue "De Minimis" or "Fair Dealing/Fair Use."

De Minimis: Producer B will argue that 15 minutes out of 120 is a small, insignificant portion. However, if those 15 minutes are the "heart" of the movie (the most important part), the court will likely reject this defense.

Fair Use (USA) / Fair Dealing (UK): This is a very difficult defense to win in commercial filmmaking. It is rarely successful when one commercial producer copies another commercial producer's work to make a profit.

Summary of Steps for Producer A:

Registration: In the USA, Producer A must have their work registered with the U.S. Copyright Office to sue for statutory damages.

Evidence: Producer A must prove that Producer B had "access" to their work (e.g., the script was sent to them, or it was publicly available) and that the works are "substantially similar."

Legal Counsel: Because these cases involve high-stakes financial damages and complex IP laws, Producer A would need to hire an Entertainment Attorney or IP Litigator.

Case analysis 2

In usa or uk movie market, when one movie producer "a" signed one partner cooperation contract to movie producer "b" to cooperate to make one movie and share half profit if their this movie can earn profit and they accept contract content and signed together. In this year, they begins to make this movie, but after three months, the movie producer "b" do not want to invest money and time and employ staffs to help movie producer "a" to continue to finish this movie, so it tells this reason to invest to help movie producer "a" to finish this movie. Then movie producer "a" sue "b" for the evidence of "b" breachs this movie cooperation partners contract, "a" need "b" to pay money compensation for "a" future estimaite profit earn and its past three months spending time and staffs salaries and entertainment facility estimate loss, whether USA or UK court can applies entertainment movie contract law to help "a" earn loss in entertainement contract law principle

In both the USA (specifically states like California or New York) and the UK, entertainment law is not a separate "branch" of law; rather, it is the application of general contract law to the specific customs and practices of the film industry. If Producer B breaches a signed cooperation agreement, Producer A has a strong legal basis to sue. Here is how the courts in these jurisdictions generally approach such a claim:

1. Breach of Contract (The Core Claim)

If the contract was signed and B stops performing their obligations (investing money, providing staff, etc.), this is a material breach.

USA: Courts look for the "four corners" of the contract. If B agreed to provide specific capital or services and failed to do so, B is liable for the damages caused by that failure.

UK: The court will look at whether B's actions constitute a "repudiatory breach," allowing A to terminate the contract and sue for damages.

2. Recovering Damages (What can A get?)

Courts generally categorize damages into two types: Reliance Damages and Expectation Damages.

A. Reliance Damages (Past Losses)

These are the easiest to prove. A is entitled to be put back in the position they were in before the contract was signed.

Staff Salaries: If A hired staff specifically for the project based on the contract, these are recoverable.

Time/Overhead: If A can prove specific "out-of-pocket" expenses (facility rentals, equipment, pre-production costs), these are generally recoverable as "reliance damages."

B. Expectation Damages (Future/Lost Profits)

This is much harder to prove in the movie industry.

The "Speculative" Problem: Courts in both the USA and UK are historically skeptical of awarding "lost profits" for movies because film success is considered highly speculative. A judge might say, "How do we know the movie would have made a profit? It might have been a box-office flop."

The "Certainty" Requirement: To win future lost profits, A must provide expert testimony (e.g., a film finance expert or distribution analyst) to prove that the profit was reasonably certain and not just a guess. If the movie was already pre-sold to distributors or had a guaranteed streaming deal, A has a much better chance of winning these damages.

3. Key Legal Principles Applied

Duty to Mitigate: In both the USA and UK, Producer A has a "duty to mitigate damages." This means A cannot just sit around and let the project die to increase the lawsuit amount. A must make a reasonable effort to find a new partner or finish the movie another way. If A fails to try to save the project, the court may reduce the compensation.

Specific Performance: It is very rare for a court to force Producer B to continue working on the movie (this is called "specific performance"). Courts generally do not like to force people to work together if the relationship has broken down. Instead, the court will almost always order monetary. compensation (damages) instead.

4. What Producer A needs to prepare

To succeed in court, Producer A needs:

The Signed Contract: Clearly outlining B's obligations (the "consideration").

Evidence of Breach: Emails, letters, or notices where B stated they would no longer invest or provide staff.

Proof of Loss: Detailed accounting records, invoices, and payroll records for the three months of work.

Expert Testimony: If claiming future lost profits, A needs a professional to testify that the project had a high probability of commercial success.

Summary Recommendation

If the contract has an "Arbitration Clause": Many entertainment contracts require disputes to be settled by an arbitrator (like JAMS or AAA in the US) rather than a public court. Check your contract.

Jurisdiction: If the contract says "Governed by the laws of California," you must use California law. If it says "England and Wales," you must use UK law.

Immediate Action: Producer A should send a formal "Notice of Breach" to Producer B immediately, demanding they cure the breach or face legal action. This is often required before filing a lawsuit.

Conclusion: Yes, the law will help A recover "out-of-pocket" losses (salaries, facility costs). However, recovering "future estimated profits" is difficult and requires strong evidence that the movie was a guaranteed financial success.

Case analysis 3

If one usa or uk restaurant "a" applies another restaurant "b" similar name for "b"restaurant band. then, the restaurant 'B" sue "a" to apply its similar name to make famous eating brand to attract many eaters choose to eat "b" restaurant similar food taste to earn high profit. Whether this restaurant "b" can apply tort law to sue this restaurant 'A" for its present profit loss , even future estimate of profit loss, due to restaurant "b" beleives that restaurant "a" had applied restaurant "b" similar restaurant name for restaurant "a" eating brand to cause restaurant "b" old eating customers feel restaurant "a" its all food taste is more nice to attract them to choose restaurant "a" to eat and replace restaurant "b" reason. Can Usa or UK court apply tort law to help restaurant "b" to sue restaurant "a"

In both the United States and the United Kingdom, the situation you described is generally not handled under general "tort law" (like negligence), but rather under specific areas of law called Intellectual Property (IP) and Unfair Competition law.

If Restaurant B wants to sue Restaurant A for using a similar name to steal customers and profit, they would typically use the following legal frameworks:

1. The Legal Grounds for the Lawsuit

In the United States:

Trademark Infringement: If Restaurant B has registered its name as a trademark, they can sue under the Lanham Act. They must prove that Restaurant A's name is likely to cause "consumer confusion"—meaning customers are tricked into thinking Restaurant A is actually Restaurant B or affiliated with them.

Unfair Competition (Passing Off): Even if the name isn't registered, Restaurant B can sue for "unfair competition." This covers situations where a business tries to "pass off" their goods as those of another to deceive the public.

In the United Kingdom:

Passing Off: This is the primary common law tort used in the UK for this situation. To win a "passing off" claim, Restaurant B must prove three things (the "Classical Trinity"):

Goodwill: Restaurant B has a reputation and a customer base.

Misrepresentation: Restaurant A has deceived the public into believing their goods/services are those of Restaurant B.

Damage: Restaurant B has suffered (or is likely to suffer) financial loss because of this deception.

2. Can Restaurant B sue for Profit Loss?

Yes. If Restaurant B wins the lawsuit, they can seek "damages" (monetary compensation). This includes:

Past Profit Loss: Restaurant B can present accounting evidence showing how much profit they lost during the time Restaurant A was using the similar name.

Future Estimated Loss: Courts can award "prospective damages" if Restaurant B can prove that the damage to their brand reputation will continue to affect their earnings in the future.

Account of Profits: In some cases, instead of asking for their own lost profits, Restaurant B can ask the court to force Restaurant A to "hand over" the profits they made while using the infringing name.

3. The Challenges (What Restaurant B must prove)

It is not enough for Restaurant B to simply say, "They used a similar name and I lost money." They must prove:

Consumer Confusion: They must show that customers are actually going to Restaurant A because they think it is Restaurant B. If the names are similar but the branding, location, and style are totally different, the court might rule that no reasonable customer would be confused.

Causation: Restaurant B must prove that the loss of profit is directly linked to the name confusion, not just because Restaurant A happens to have better food or better prices. If customers prefer Restaurant A simply because the food tastes better, that is fair competition, not a legal tort.

Reputation: Restaurant B must prove they had an established reputation before Restaurant A opened.

Summary

Restaurant B does not need to rely on general "tort law" (like a car accident claim). Instead, they would hire an IP lawyer to file a lawsuit for Trademark Infringement or Passing Off.

If they can prove that Restaurant A intentionally used a similar name to deceive customers and that this deception caused a measurable loss of business, the courts in both the US and UK have the power to order Restaurant A to:

Stop using the name (an Injunction).

Pay for the lost profits (Damages).

Pay for the legal fees of Restaurant B.